2020:
The Year That Changed the World

Sophia Montagna

All rights reserved. © 2024 Sophia Montagna

No part of this document may be reproduced, sold, stored in or introduced into a retrieval system, or transmitted, in any form or by any means (electronic, mechanical, photocopying, recording or otherwise), without prior permission.

Disclaimer: This book is based on the author's personal experience of 2020 and, additionally, a wide range of media sources for which the author has no liability. The sources used have been published, formed part of national news articles and are available to be viewed online where they still exist. All information correct at time of publication.

ISBN-13: 9798340804372

British Cataloguing Publication Data
A catalogue record of this book is available from The British Library.

Also available on Kindle from Amazon

Contents

Preface 5

Introduction 7

Chapter 1: Happy New Year 9

Chapter 2: Keeping It Hidden 13

Chapter 3: The Unknown Becoming Known 17

Chapter 4: Midst of a Crisis 23

Chapter 5: And the Rollercoaster Begins 29

Chapter 6: The Long Road Ahead 37

Chapter 7: The Good and The Bad 45

Chapter 8: The Ongoing Picture 55

Chapter 9: Four Months Into Lockdown 65

Chapter 10: Summertime! 73

Chapter 11: The Conspiracies Begin 81

Chapter 12: The Autumn Blues 85

Chapter 13: Is This Over Yet? 91

Chapter 14: It's Christmas, and 2021 is Upon Us! 97

Acknowledgements 101

About the Author 103

References 105

Preface

This book came about during a time that felt surreal, a time that didn't quite feel right, a time of uncertainty coupled with tremendous fear. This was my opportunity to write about an event that will make history in years to come; I wanted to allow my children and future generations to read about the events that unfolded in 2020 and beyond.

In most countries across the globe, the COVID pandemic became the biggest national emergency. It appeared from nowhere and, in a blink of an eye, we were subjected to national lockdowns that took away our routines, our joys and pleasures, our way of living and our freedom. Everything we once knew as normal suddenly felt like a previous life.

It was a year that changed everything for millions of people around the world. This is my insight into our world in 2020.

Introduction

The chapters in this book represent the whole of 2020, and each chapter delves deeper into the events we lived through. This book encompasses much of what I remember and what was represented in the media, giving us an opportunity to look back at the rollercoaster of ups and downs that created our new reality.

Let's begin at the very start of the year 2020...

Chapter 1
Happy New Year

2020 commences with the sound of fireworks, the pulling of party poppers, happy people across the globe jumping up and down with excitement as they welcome in the new year. For many, it is the most awaited night of the year: we plan what to do, what to wear and arrange transport to venues; perhaps it is a stay-at-home type of affair with friends and family round for a party; maybe it's just a quiet night in watching the New Year celebrations on the television.

As people wake up late on the 1st of January 2020, some after a heavy night of celebrating, the new year is upon us. The past year may have been brilliant, with weddings, births, new jobs and new relationships, or perhaps not so good a year, with illnesses, deaths, job loss or divorce. However, as we embrace the end of the old year we look forward to the year ahead – and some of us may put that great plan in place... yes, I am talking about our great New Year's resolutions. The aim is to decide what you want to do and go about achieving it... If only it was that simple! We get so far and soon the dreaded thing occurs – yes, we cheat on that New Year commitment and swiftly move on with life and forget about it.

2020 was the start of a new decade: even more of a reason to celebrate and be excited for the year ahead. I certainly had big plans, including the opportunity to take part in my very first pantomime on stage in the West End of London. Snow White – who doesn't like a bit of Disney!

I was working with a great bunch of passionate people and being on stage in London was amazing in itself. Not only that, but funds were being raised for the Springboard Charity, which supports individuals facing barriers to employment to fall in love with hospitality, leisure and tourism. It felt amazing doing something so enjoyable but also rewarding, to be helping and supporting other people.

The three nights on stage in January were incredible; I started the year off with a bang! I felt like I was an actress in a full-blown theatre production... Well, technically it was. It's something I will definitely do again and it was one of those things – okay, maybe more of a New Year's resolution – to do something I had never done before, and I am proud to say that I stuck to it and achieved it.

One of the other major things happening for me in 2020 was a scheduled operation. In what was already a hectic year, I wasn't looking forward to the many hours in surgery and the six weeks of recovery. I underwent surgery on 11th February and started my road to recovery as soon as I got home that day. It was the longest I had stayed at home and by the second week I was starting to get work withdrawal symptoms. However, my recovery went well and I was soon back at work.

I love my job in Human Resources. We sometimes get called the 'People Police' but this certainly isn't the case. I thrive on helping others by encouraging learning and development, inspiring others to achieve their highest potential. Additionally, I enjoy being there for individuals who really just want to talk, especially as I am a Mental Health First Aider. Gone are the days when HR were seen to be scary people you really didn't want to be seeing at any point in your career (although I am sure a few still exist).

As a family, we had a holiday booked to Sicily in August. My cousin was getting married there and this would be the first time in many years that we would all be together in celebration. In addition, my mum, in remission from cancer, was celebrating her 60th birthday with a big party.

I was also looking forward to my next belly dance show, in November. Every week I attend classes with a group of amazing women who are passionate about dance and the great benefits it brings. Our annual show is the time of year when we wear all those amazing, sparkly, colourful costumes and perform to our family and friends – but this year was our 10-year anniversary show, so it would be extra special. It was definitely something to look forward to.

2020 was set to be an exciting year for me. However, no one could have predicted what was to come.

Chapter 2
Keeping It Hidden

While I was at home recovering from surgery, I had plenty of time to catch up on the news and see what was going on in the world. There were stories about an infection that had been detected in China but I didn't pay too much attention to it as it wasn't breaking news and China is a fair few thousand miles away, so I didn't really feel concerned.

During this time, my family and I were planning our trip to Sicily and there were lots of messages going back and forth with flight options and details of hotels along the south east coast. By 24th February, we had decided on flights and a hotel, and we got them booked. Six months and we would be on holiday... how exciting!

More and more appeared on the news regarding the virus in China but again, it didn't really worry me. How wrong could I have been?

While the rest of the world was getting ready for Christmas and New Year's Eve celebrations, little did we know that there was a hidden infection looming in China: an infection that could be insignificant and managed within Wuhan, the area it originated – or that could be so dangerous that many people's lives would be at risk. At this time, we were none the wiser.

The infection was first identified in China back on 8th December 2019 when the first case emerged, alleged to have originated from the Huanan Seafood Market. China kept the information low key and there was no mention of it in the news in the UK. However, it appears that on 31st

December, China informed the World Health Organization (WHO) that there were cases of pneumonia in Wuhan, Hubei Province. It seems there was not enough information or medical understanding about what was causing this bout of pneumonia within residents.

By 1st January 2020, the WHO moved into emergency mode to deal with a major disease outbreak, which was very much kept quiet by the Chinese government. Following the report of the infection, the Huanan Seafood Market was shut down. Known as a 'wet market', it sells meat, poultry and seafood alongside live animals such as dogs, chickens, pigs and snakes. There was clearly a link between the market and the suspected infection that caused concern for the WHO.

For some of us in Europe, the buying of live animals for consumption is beyond comprehension and in most cases there would be disgust about such behaviour, especially with animals considered much-loved pets here. In any case, the market being shut down suggested there was a risk that this new infection was linked to the selling of live animals. We were not sure how well regulated the animal market was, and there was a risk to those buying that there could be underlying disease in the animals that could cause 'zoonotic' diseases, where they transfer from animals to humans.

Back in 2003 there was an outbreak of SARS (Severe Acute Respiratory Syndrome), which also originated in China. This virus infected 8,000 people worldwide and killed nearly 800; the cause was suspected to be bats infecting animals that were later bought in the wet markets. Those who were infected had symptoms including a cough, shortness of breath, fever, headache and diarrhoea, and this was passed on from person to person.

The SARS pandemic ended in July 2003; however,

circumstantial evidence showed transmission from animals to humans. We were now in 2020 and, potentially, we had a new case of animal-to-human transmission – and yet since 2003 the Chinese government had continued to allow the buying and consumption of animals. It wasn't until 24th February 2020, following the outbreak of this new infection, that they finally banned the buying, selling and eating of wildlife.

On 4th January 2020, the WHO reported on social media that there had been a rise in pneumonia cases in Wuhan, but no deaths. On 7th January, the Chinese authorities confirmed that the disease had been identified as a type of coronavirus, which can cause illness ranging from a cold to more severe respiratory issues. Four days later, on 11th January, the first death was reported in Wuhan, a man in his 60s with underlying health conditions.

On 13th January, the first reported case outside of China was confirmed in Thailand. The next day, the WHO warned of the risk of a coronavirus outbreak. Soon after, on 20th January, the virus had reached the US, where a man in his 30s had a confirmed case after returning from a trip to Wuhan. By late January, there were cases in China, Thailand, the USA, Japan and South Korea.

This was the beginning of what was to come, not only for China but for the rest of the world.

Chapter 3
The Unknown Becoming Known

While we were continuing to live a normal life in the UK, there was a virus spreading with cases now in Australia, Canada, France and Malaysia. In China, there were 769 new cases; globally, there were 2,801 cases – and 80 deaths. It was starting to look like something more serious was looming upon us.

The World Health Organization (WHO) held an emergency meeting with authorities across the world but on 22nd January a decision was made not to advise the WHO Director General to declare the outbreak a public health emergency of international concern, even though there had been human-to-human transmission of the virus.

Although there was no public declaration about the virus, on 23rd January the city of Wuhan shut down public transportation, closing airports and railway stations to prevent the spread. It was now in lockdown: there was no travel in or out of the city, cars were banned from roads, shops were shut except for those selling food; the streets of Wuhan were as silent as they could be. Later that day other cities – Ezhou and Huanggang – also went into lockdown.

By 28th January, there were 5,974 cases and 132 deaths in China and a global total of over 6,000 cases. Whatever this virus was, it was spreading fast and wide. On 31st January, BBC News reported two confirmed cases in the UK and there potentially being more, as 83 Britons had been evacuated from Wuhan.

It was on 30th January that the WHO Director General,

Tedros Adhanom Ghebreyesus, finally declared the 2019-nCoV outbreak a public health emergency of international concern. The name was an interim one; however, it was described as an 'acute respiratory disease', something similar, it appears, to SARS in 2003.

Information was slowly coming in from China. They confirmed a clinical trial of an antiviral drug previously tested in patients with Ebola and, with cases now at 20,438, they built a new hospital in just 10 days to treat patients with 2019-nCoV; this opened on 3rd February.

Although news reports were starting to arrive on the situation in China, it was still very much something that was not discussed or watched on the news in the UK. We have all done it – we either don't watch the news at all, or we read it on our phones but in most cases if it doesn't affect us then we don't have an interest. This outbreak certainly wasn't a topic of conversation for me. I knew I was going in for my surgery in a week and I didn't have any concerns about the effects of this virus.

On 5th February, ten passengers on a cruise ship docked at Yokohama, Japan tested positive for the virus and all passengers were put into lockdown on the ship. Global cases had now reached over 28,000 and some countries with weak health systems were worrying about whether they could cope. Japan announced a $10-million contribution to the 2019-nCoV outbreak response fund, which would support those countries.

Meanwhile, a local doctor in Wuhan, Li Wenliang, died from the virus. Wenliang had tried to raise the alarm on 2019-nCoV in December. Because his concerns were not taken on board at the time, there was anger in China towards the government, who were prompted to apologise to his family. Wenliang was hailed a hero.

The Diamond Princess cruise ship in Japan became a focal point in the news when a total of 61 passengers were confirmed to have the virus. Still in lockdown, all 3,700 passengers had been tested for the virus and news reports suggested that the number of passengers becoming infected was worrying and the conditions on board the ship were 'violating all infection control principles'. We witnessed footage from passengers who were confined to their cabins for a fourteen-day quarantine period, particularly an older couple from the UK. They described their daily routine of walking up and down the cabin to get some exercise and explained that their meals were delivered to them every day. It certainly wasn't the experience they had wished for as they embarked on a luxury cruise that ended up being a breeding ground for the virus.

On 10th February, the UK's health department declared 2019-nCoV an 'imminent threat' to public health which would potentially force people into quarantine. The next day, the WHO assigned the novel coronavirus its new name – COVID-19 – and said there could be a vaccine in about 18 months. With cases rising significantly across the world daily and deaths starting to rise, there was an imminent threat to all countries globally. What were we really dealing with here?

The death toll was now over 800, surpassing the SARS pandemic in 2003, which claimed 773 people's lives. As research forums started to form and information was gathered on infection prevention, the world was slowly coming together as we experienced the very early stages of a pandemic.

It was now the middle of February, and we were slowly starting to hear more about the virus – though not as much as we should have. As I sat on the couch, wearing compression garments after my surgery and spending full days sleeping, watching TV and getting up to stretch my legs every few hours, I thought it was the perfect time to finalise our travel itinerary. We had plans to start in Rome and then travel down to the south to Sicily. I watched a lot of news and daytime TV (which, surprisingly, I quite enjoyed) and I never got the impression that this virus was going to be any more serious than your normal seasonal flu.

More statistics came through over the coming days. A total of 175 passengers on the Diamond Princess cruise ship had tested positive, Egypt reported its first case, France and Taiwan reported their first deaths, and China published a paper communicating that there were more than 44,000 confirmed COVID-19 cases there. The report illustrated that COVID-19 was not as deadly as other coronaviruses; however, mortality rates increased in older patients. At this stage, reported cases were only laboratory confirmed, though this did change to include clinically confirmed cases via chest imaging.

The virus was continuing to spread like wildfire, and the WHO was concerned by the rapid speed COVID-19 was reaching all parts of the world. Cases were now in Lebanon and Israel. The death toll surpassed 2,000 worldwide and the WHO Director General stated: "This virus is very dangerous, and it's public enemy number one. But it's not being treated as such, and one important indicator is the response, especially to financing the response." Countries around the world were preparing for the worst and reviewing their health systems in readiness of what was to come. African countries confirmed they were 66% ready, which was not enough considering the shocking rate of how fast the virus was spreading. The European Commission announced a new aid package of 232 million euros for global preparedness and response to COVID-19.

As leaders across the globe watched China go through the worst of it first, they were preparing for the unthinkable. This was now getting rather serious.

On 26th February, Greece, Georgia, Norway, Romania, Pakistan, Denmark, Estonia, Netherlands and Brazil all reported their first case of COVID-19. The WHO raised the global risk of spread from 'high' to 'very high', and WHO's Dr Michael Ryan sent a stark warning: "This is a reality check for every government on the planet. Wake up. Get ready. This virus may be on its way, and you need to be ready." We were now starting to see the reality of what was coming. South Korea with 3,736 cases and Italy with 1,128 cases had the most cases outside China, as of 1st March 2020. In the UK, a £46-million package for the COVID-19 response was announced.

By the start of March, we were heading into the unknown. There was a rush to find out more about the virus and clinical trials were taking place. Fast-tracking of the development of a vaccine was in full force and there were questions about how long the virus would last, what impact it would have on the economy and health systems... the questions went on and on. Some of the headlines in the news in March included 'Coronavirus: The month everything changed', 'UK deaths rise by more than 100 in a day', and 'Number of global COVID-19 cases passes 750,000 with the death toll over 36,000'. March 2020 definitely was the month where everything changed – changes that would see us experiencing the unthinkable.

Chapter 4
Midst of a Crisis

After nearly two weeks at home, I started to get back to work and into the swing of things again after my surgery. I was so excited to get out of the house, to drive, to see my colleagues and get my brain working again. I wanted to skip back into work but my legs wouldn't allow me to do that, so a gentle walk it was.

On 2nd March, I input an entry into my phone's diary that said, "Starting to hear about COVID". I am not sure what made me want to do that, but I felt it would be good to make a note. A week later, I had a hospital appointment. I was a little nervous because of the news headlines but I still went ahead and again I entered a diary note saying, "Covid is getting worse". I must say, I have good intuition and somehow my gut was telling me to make notes; I was starting to sense that this was much bigger than we were being told.

More information had come in and the WHO moved closer to declaring the COVID-19 outbreak a pandemic. As the world continued to prepare and respond to COVID-19, this was starting to become our reality. It wasn't long before the WHO officially declared the outbreak a pandemic. On 11th March, the WHO Director General stated that "We are deeply concerned both by the alarming levels of spread and severity and the alarming levels of inaction. We have called every day for countries to take urgent and aggressive action."

We were now looking at over 100 countries reporting cases

of COVID-19, with the total cases surpassing 100,000. Europe was now the epicentre of the pandemic with more reported cases and deaths than the rest of the world. We watched the situation unfold in Italy, the worst hit country in Europe. The news headlines on 10th March were a warning of things to come as Italy went into full lockdown to prevent the spread of the virus, which had started in the Lombardy region. As we watched in horror, we witnessed the true extent of what our lives could potentially be like in a few weeks' time: hundreds of people dying every day, an insight into what was going on in the hospitals, the strain it was putting on the healthcare system, exhausted doctors and nurses sleeping wherever they could find a space, the marks on their faces from the personal protective equipment (PPE), hearing and seeing people struggling to breathe as they let ventilators do the work for them. It was horrendous – and this is when it really hit home. We were dealing with the unthinkable and unimaginable. What was going on?

Italy being in lockdown meant that no one could go out apart from buying essential food. You were not allowed to get any exercise outside or see your friends or family; all businesses were shut, and the police roamed the streets waiting to catch those breaking the law. Funerals were not permitted and therefore the many people who had sadly died from the virus were being put in churches and refrigerated lorries as space was running out in the morgues. Families were unable to say goodbye to their loved ones because of the risk of catching the virus, which meant thousands of people died alone as they struggled to breathe. Pneumonia was one of the biggest causes of death with this virus, and it was a slippery road for those who got to that stage.

It was shocking for the rest of the world to watch a nation fall to its knees, to see busy tourist cities turn into ghost towns and hear the fear in the voices of residents who were scared of what was going on. This lockdown was different to that in China. From the onset we hadn't had much information on what was happening in China. Seeing Italy go into lockdown was a turning point for countries across the globe.

Lombardy, a northern region in Italy with its capital being Milan, is a global hub of fashion and finance. It has the most advanced health care system in the whole of Italy, and it was bearing the brunt of COVID-19. As hospital beds started to run out, news coverage showed senior doctors warning the world of what was to come and stating we needed to be prepared. Doctors who had retired came back into service to help out; sadly, some of them caught the virus and died. Healthcare workers were now at risk of contracting the virus whilst dealing with patients. They were putting their lives on the line and their courage and determination was shown on all the news channels.

Personal protective equipment (PPE) was enforced; masks and gloves were worn by those going out to buy food. All precautions had to be taken to reduce the risk of catching this deadly virus, which was taking life after life, day after day. The Italians showed us a true picture of the life they were living – and, potentially, we were only a couple of weeks away from going through the same. The proud and patriotic Italians sang from their balconies whilst in lockdown, filling our screens with scenes of music, solidarity and hope. Talented musicians played guitars, trumpets, saxophones and beautiful singers filled the streets with their amazing voices. It was truly heart-warming to see everyone come together, lifting each other's spirits at this sad and scary time.

My family come from Sicily and at this moment I truly felt the goosebumps as I remembered where I am from, my culture, my heritage and my second home. I immediately thought about my family in Italy, being told to stay at home for what could be a long period of time while the Italian government tried to battle this virus. I thought about the health of my loved ones, and hoped none of them were unwell or, worse, had lost their life. I sent messages to my family and checked in on them. Thankfully they were safe at home, adhering to the lockdown measures and social distancing if they did have to go out to the shops.

My mind came back home as I witnessed what was going on in the world. I worried for my mother, who had fought cancer the year before and had a low immune system; I worried about the impact this could have on her. I started to think about what life would be like if we were in lockdown. What would happen with work and my employment? What would I do at home? How long would it be before I could see my friends and family? The questions were endless. However, we weren't there yet, so I decided to concentrate on the here and now and take precautions.

It was the middle of March and cases had now reached Puerto Rico, Sudan, Venezuela, Kenya, St Lucia and many more countries. Cases in Africa were on the rise: a week earlier there were only 27 confirmed cases and now there were 273, a 73% increase, and it was continuing to rise. Infections and deaths outside China surpassed those within China and there was now a rise in social distancing measures, with schools closing and large events being cancelled.

On 19th March, cases of COVID-19 surpassed 200,000 globally. It had taken three months to reach 100,000 and only 12 days to reach the next 100,000. More and more funding was being provided by the World Bank Group, and the WHO was calling on countries to "urgently scale up aggressive measures" to combat the spread. On this same day, Wuhan – the city where it all began – reported no new cases.

COVID-19 seemed to have hit older people significantly, with many of those who died in Italy from the older generation. However, the WHO Director General confirmed that data from many countries showed that the under 50s made up a significant proportion of patients requiring hospitalization. This virus was affecting everyone of all ages and the message I heard many times was that anyone could catch it. Initially, this wasn't taken seriously. However, as time went on, the media started reporting it every day and the news headlines were full of COVID-19 stories – and panic started to set in.

While I was getting used to being back at work, I had the sudden realisation that I could potentially be back home for a significant period of time, so I started to get things together. I went to the shops and bought everything I may need, including toiletries and make up. I also thought about things I could do, and ordered some diamond painting sets, which are a mix of cross stitch and paint by numbers. At work we were starting to implement new procedures, so I worked with my Manager to provide staff training on COVID-19. Bacterial wipes and sanitizers were provided in all areas and we were starting to socially distance ourselves in the workplace. A strong message we sent out to our teams was about the importance of washing hands; posters were put up and we started to use sanitizer like it was a sacred gel. I never imagined having to use a significant amount of alcohol on my hands; I'd have preferred it to be in a nice glass of Baileys or in one of my favourite cocktails.

This was starting to become real. We were heading in the

same direction as China, Italy and many other countries across the world. We weren't in lockdown yet – but it was coming. I watched the news every day like it was mandatory, and I absorbed everything that was being said. The next day at work we would discuss when the business may need to close if we were heading into a lockdown. By this point, our customers were slowing leaving as more and more people watched what was happening in the world.

We were close – very close – to witnessing the weirdest and scariest time in our lives. The anxiety was building, a bit like when you are on a big rollercoaster. As you go up, you can hear the clunking until you reach the top. We were now heading into the drop – the drop of the unknown, as we couldn't see down below but could only imagine what it would be like from what we had seen elsewhere.

Were we ready?

No, we certainly weren't...

Chapter 5
And the Rollercoaster Begins

It was nearly the end of March, and I could feel lockdown coming as cases continued to rise globally. There was frustration in the UK as people complained about why we were not in lockdown already. Our prime minister, Boris Johnson had been relying on scientific data and was strategically planning when lockdown would begin. Italy warned us over and over again to be prepared and they were also unsure about why we were not in lockdown at this time. More and more posts were appearing on social media as anxiety rose and people started to worry about catching the virus. I witnessed people arguing with each other on social media about what Boris Johnson was doing; clearly the frustration was getting to people. Then it all came to a head when the panic buying started.

I had never witnessed anything so crazy in my life. People were queuing to get into supermarkets to buy toilet rolls – and not just one packet, but several packs. Confusion set in as to why toilet roll was one of the must-have items. COVID-19's main symptoms were a new, dry cough and a temperature, yet people were stocking up on toilet roll. Other items on the panic-buying list were flour, painkillers, tinned food and the obvious sanitiser and hand wash, and all these items began to be sold out everywhere. The weekly shop was not the same anymore as items flew off the shelves. The meat aisles were empty, as was the cereal aisle, and most essential items had disappeared off the shelves within minutes. I could not find eggs in my search for them and that was the one food item I really wanted, so I started to look at local farms in my area to see if any were going there. People were panic buying as if they couldn't ever buy food again – even though we were told not to panic buy as there was enough in the supply chain for everyone.

The message didn't really sink in, and it continued for weeks – and not only in the UK. The toilet roll phenomena reached far and wide, to the USA and Australia, where footage was shown of people fighting over toilet rolls. By this point, I thought the world had gone mad; it was unreal. However, considering the idea of a lockdown had been presented to the nation and the media were only concentrating on COVID-19, it was no surprise that this was happening. Luckily, the supermarkets did finally put in buying restrictions on key items and this allowed for things to be available again, albeit in very small quantities.

It was now 23rd March and the day we suspected would arrive did arrive. At 5pm, the UK went into lockdown. We were advised that we could only go out for essential food items and one hour of exercise a day, and work continued only for those who were essential workers. This was it: we had come to a halt in our daily activities. All businesses were shut except for supermarkets, petrol stations and takeaways; you could also still attend necessary medical appointments. Aside from that, you could not go anywhere; you could not see your family or go to their houses. We were now confined to our homes for at least three weeks to combat the spread of COVID-19.

Elsewhere, India announced a lockdown of 21 days for the country's 1.3 billion residents and cases surpassed 400,000 globally. It had taken three months to reach 100,000, twelve days to reach 200,000, three days to reach 300,000 and just two days to reach 400,000. The numbers were frightening, and the death toll on a daily basis was starting to show everyone how serious the virus was.

On 25th March, the United Nations launched a $2 billion global humanitarian response which would assist vulnerable countries and fund equipment, medical supplies, hand-washing stations and much more. The UN Secretary, General Antonio Guterres, said: "COVID-19 is menacing the whole of humanity – and so the whole of humanity must fight back. Individual country responses are not going to be enough."

Meanwhile, in the UK we were settling into our new reality – one of uncertainty, worry and fear – as we watched to see what happened. I never imagined I would be writing this, but here is a list of everything that changed:

- Schools were shut and parents took on the role of teachers as they started home schooling
- Non-essential shops and businesses were all shut
- Popular fast food and coffee outlets such as McDonalds, Burger King and Costa Coffee were all shut
- Parks were shut
- All restaurants were shut
- All entertainment venues, cinemas, theatres and hotels were shut
- Supermarkets put tape down on floors to direct people through aisles and communicated the 2m distance rule
- Queues appeared outside supermarkets as there was a limited number of people who could shop at any one time
- Sports season was put on hold

- Concerts, festivals and entertainment events were all cancelled
- Weddings and celebrations were cancelled
- Funerals were limited to 10 people, and all had to socially distance themselves
- Churches were shut; no masses
- No socialising with anyone outside your household
- Shortage of masks, gowns and gloves for front-line workers
- People were wearing gloves and masks when going to do their shopping
- Panic buying continued and shelves were bare
- People were disinfecting their shopping items before putting them in the fridge
- Roads were empty, towns were like ghost towns
- Borders had closed and only essential travel was permitted
- Airlines stopped flying as most other countries closed their borders
- Shortage of ventilators in hospitals
- Post and parcels were being disinfected once people received them
- We were told to stay at home
- Aside from essential workers, people were now off work

The social distancing rules were now officially in place as we tried to avoid close contact with people. Daily walks involved looking at the path ahead and planning your next move if someone was coming towards you... "I will move as far left as I can and try not to walk into the road." Some of my friends mentioned how people looked at each other weirdly as they passed each other; they could see the thoughts going through their minds... "Hmm, do you have it?" Luckily, where I lived in Bedfordshire, everyone was friendly and we smiled at each other as we walked past. Everyone did their bit to give people space. We were all in it together, after all.

The trip to the supermarket became interesting. We queued and had to keep a 2-metre distance; pavements had markers, so we knew where to stand; and we were more and more concerned with the hygiene of the trolleys and baskets we touched. My routine visit involved me bringing anti-bacterial wet wipes and as I took a trolley I gave the handle a nice wipe down; the guidance provided was to do this for 30 seconds. The interesting bit was when we took our shopping home. You didn't know who had touched the items before you, so people resorted to 'washing their shopping', some in soapy water and others with wipes. I personally used wipes and I made sure I disinfected the worktop afterwards.

Obviously, there were things you couldn't wash in soapy water, like your fresh vegetables and your fresh parsley pot. Some people told me they didn't buy items that couldn't be washed for fear of catching the virus. The trip to the supermarket had changed, and there we were thinking of everything we could do to avoid catching this deadly virus. It was life-changing.

We were living a life that involved staying at home, taking one hour to walk or undertake exercise outside, and a trip to the supermarket for essential food. Days and days passed. The initial novelty of a few weeks off work was great for some; however, the boredom started to set in as we were soon getting used to a life at home. I kept myself busy during this time. I had already written a list of everything I had to do at home – and what better time to do it! I saw many posts from friends and family doing exactly the same thing: cleaning, cleaning and more cleaning. It was when the cleaning had been completed that we found ourselves looking for other things to do.

Something I saw more and more was people baking, making cakes and biscuits, and I saw lovely garden projects and decorating. People started to use the time to do all the things they hadn't had a chance to do before. A couple of friends said they could finally go through the list of things their partners had given them to do, many months before; however, this time there was no way of getting out of it. I had finished all my cleaning and moved onto card making, which I have always enjoyed. I also created diamond paintings, and I read more than at any other time in my life. I started meditating, as a friend of mine introduced me to the 21-day Deepak Chopra challenge, which really changed my thought process and view of life. I was dancing nearly every day and took part in belly dance challenges with the lovely ladies in our group. It wasn't so bad for the initial three weeks of lockdown.

On 26th March, the UK started a 'Clap for the National Health Service (NHS)', which was to thank all our doctors, nurses, ambulance service and all others on the front line for their hard work and commitment during COVID-19. The clap took place on Thursday evenings at 8pm and saw the whole nation come together as people stood outside their houses and clapped for the NHS. It was amazing to see so many people take part and stay committed to doing this every week; we really were a nation that was pulling together and appreciating what our great people were doing on the front line.

It was now 27th March and, after a scientific brief, the WHO confirmed that droplets on surfaces and objects from an infected person were the main route of transmission for COVID-19. There was also the worry of airborne transmission, which was much harder to manage. We were guided to wash our hands for 20 seconds and soon after we had songs to wash our hands to... Yes... Wash your hands for 20 seconds while singing *Happy Birthday*. I am not sure if that was to make us feel better, as we found ourselves washing our hands constantly, so much so that hand cream was another essential item as our hands dried out from the mass use of alcohol.

On this day the WHO also announced the Solidarity Trial to go ahead in Norway and Spain as they compared the effectiveness of drug combinations against COVID-19. The WHO Director General said this was a "historic trial that will dramatically cut the time needed to generate robust evidence about what drugs work". There was a lot of funding going into trials at this time – and then we found out that our prime minister, Boris Johnson had tested positive for COVID-19.

Boris was isolated at Number 10 Downing Street in London and still continued to run the country, with help from his aides, whilst in isolation, which was a period of 14 days. We never imagined our prime minister catching the virus, just as he was drilling into the nation how important it was that we stay at home and socially distance ourselves. It showed that any one of us could catch it.

On 28th March, COVID-19 cases worldwide surpassed 600,000. On this day, Spain and Italy had the highest number of deaths in a day, with Spain recording 832 deaths and Italy recording 889 deaths. The global death toll had now surpassed 30,000. Every day we were seeing similar figures, which was crazy – all those poor families dealing with the deaths of loved ones. At the epicentre of the virus in China, Wuhan was now slowly easing their lockdown restrictions as the number of deaths and cases were dropping.

Every country was at a different stage of the virus and the world was eagerly watching as governments planned their next move. Lockdowns were interpreted differently across the globe. In Nairobi, a 13-year-old was standing on a balcony at his home when he was shot by police as they enforced a national curfew to prevent the spread of the virus. Sadly, the reality was becoming evident all over the world.

Chapter 6
The Long Road Ahead

April 2020 was upon us. It was nearly five months since Wuhan reported their first case; however, a news article in March had reported that the first case of COVID-19 was actually in November 2019, according to reports from unpublished Chinese government data. The post in the *South China Morning Post* identified that "at least 266 people contracted the virus last year and came under medical surveillance, and the earliest case was 17 November 2019 – weeks before authorities announced the emergence of the virus." Although the Chinese government had certainly tried to contain the virus, they had not initially reported the outbreak and, as the months passed, many different theories emerged.

The ExCeL exhibition centre in London, which is normally used for events, conferences and expos, had been temporarily converted into the NHS Nightingale Hospital. BBC News reported that the hospital, built in just 9 days, had the capacity for 80 wards of 4,000 beds, fully equipped with oxygen and ventilators. If it reached capacity, it would be the largest hospital in the world. What was interesting was that every ward was named after a different British doctor, nurse or medical professional: a great way to recognise the amazing health professionals we have in the UK. Built with the help of soldiers, the hospital opened on 3rd April, just in time for the predicted peak of cases in the UK.

Work continued behind the scenes to develop a vaccine; however, this was only half the battle: once we did have a vaccine, it would have to be manufactured for billions of people across the globe. It wasn't going to be an easy task. Not only that, but the global economic impact had been estimated to be between $2 trillion and $4 trillion, according to the Asian Development Bank. This was based on a 3–6-month period; however, the impact could be higher if the pandemic wasn't contained by the end of September. It seemed there was a long road ahead of us before any normality could return.

On 6th April, it was reported that 90% of students globally were affected by school closures. That equated to 1.5 billion children, according to the WHO. We witnessed parents taking on schooling, with many saying they appreciated teachers more now than they did before as they felt the pressure. Some enjoyed it and others not so much; it certainly put a strain on those parents who had to work from home. Children of key workers were allowed to attend school under strict conditions in the UK, which helped whilst their parents were working.

On this same day, Boris Johnson, struggling with his breathing, was moved to Intensive Care as his condition worsened. Media coverage showed police outside St Thomas's Hospital in London as Boris was looked after by nurses and doctors, and this helped many people understand the wrath of COVID-19. We were all waiting patiently for further news as conversation among friends and family turned to "God, can you imagine if Boris Johnson dies?"

Life was surreal. I would wake up some days and think, "Are we really going through this? Is this really happening?" I felt I had to take a moment to acknowledge what was happening in the world and the inspiration to write this book came shortly after. "What a way to mark a historic time in our life!" I thought. "I have to do this, even if it's just for my children to read one day." Instead of putting pen to paper, I went straight in with fingers on keys.

We saw more and more of what life was like on the front line for our key workers – nurses and doctors who were dealing with COVID-19 patients. They were risking their lives every day to look after the nation. However, the WHO identified a global shortage of 5.9 million nurses, predominantly in Africa, Southeast Asia, Latin America and the Eastern Mediterranean. Not only did we have a shortage of nurses, but we also anticipated a shortage of hospital beds, and this prompted the UK to build a new hospital, just as they did in Wuhan.

On 8th April, China lifted their lockdown on the city of Wuhan, which is where the outbreak allegedly began back in November 2019. The US president, Donald Trump, threatened to withhold funds from the WHO as the agency had "missed the call" on the pandemic response. Director General, Tedros Adhanom Ghebreyesus of the WHO responded with, "If you don't want many more body bags, then you refrain from politicizing it." There was still anguish regarding how the virus developed and China's tactics of keeping it under wraps had continued to cause governments, particularly the United States, to feel disgruntled. On 11th April the United States recorded 2,000 deaths in one day. This was the highest death rate recorded by any country to date – and the death rate was only going to get worse.

Funding was constantly required to assist vulnerable countries and a further £200 million was pledged by the UK government to support UN agencies. The Asian Development Bank extended its pledge to $20 billion from its initial $6.5 billion, yet more was required to support over the months to come as further research was needed to find a vaccine.

On 14th April, the relationship between the United States and the WHO deteriorated even further as the US president Donald Trump declared he was "cutting off the nation's contributions to the World Health Organisation" as he criticised the agency for mismanaging the response. The newspapers capitalised on this with headlines such as "As Trump attacks WHO, World Bank looks for shareholder support". This put some pressure on the WHO, as the United States had supported the agency from the beginning with COVID-19 funding. The Director General of the WHO was looking at filling the financial gaps now that the US had decided to withdraw funding. Tedros Adhanom Ghebreyesus was quoted as saying, "When we are divided, the virus exploits the cracks between us. We are committed to serving the world's people and accountability for the resources with which we are entrusted. But for now, our focus, my focus, is on stopping this virus and saving lives ... WHO is getting on with the job."

By 15th April, COVID-19 cases had surpassed two million, with a rapid increase in cases in Africa. Further worry over the lack of personal protective equipment was impacting the response in African countries. The death toll was rising significantly every day, and more suspicion was placed on the Chinese government as they revised the death toll in Wuhan from 2,579 to 3,869. This was an increase of 50%, which raised further questions on the validity of their data.

Back in the UK, we were now three weeks into our lockdown, and we were waiting for this to be extended. Whilst the supermarkets stocked up their shelves as panic buying began to decrease, we started to look at ways we could come together and support not only the National Health Service but also a special man named Captain Tom

Moore. In early April, Captain Tom Moore, who was 99 years old, decided he wanted to raise £1,000 for the NHS by walking up and down his garden 100 times before his 100th birthday. The *Guardian* newspaper reported that "he felt inspired by the treatment he received from the NHS after breaking his hip and for his skin cancer".

Captain Tom Moore was soon live on the BBC *Breakfast* programme. As a former British Army Officer, he proudly wore his medals as he walked up and down his garden with his walking frame –. The news coverage increased every day with donations on Tom's fundraising page going from £1,000 to £1,000,000-plus; the nation was in complete awe of this man. Birthday cards started to flock in for Tom as he neared his 100th birthday, and he and his family couldn't believe he was now a very famous man appearing on all the news channels.

On 16th April, Captain Tom Moore finished his challenge. He had already raised over £20 million and had received at least 160,000 birthday cards – including one from me. I went all out to personalise my birthday card to Tom. I made little medals, just like he had on his blazer, and I put his name on the front; I really wanted it to stand out. When photos emerged of his thousands of cards, which were set up in a school hall, I soon realised mine was not so easy to find. I felt proud it was there anyhow, and that he'd had the opportunity to read it.

What an amazing achievement for Captain Tom Moore – and more was to come, when Captain Tom became Colonel Tom as he was promoted to an honorary role by the British Army. The *Guardian* reported, "Boris Johnson wished him a happy birthday, the Queen sent her customary telegram, and the wartime Spitfire and Hurricane flew over Marston Moretaine." Colonel Tom raised a whopping £32 million, which was absolutely outstanding, and this was now going to the NHS, which continued to provide 'high quality care for all, now and for future generations'.

Back to the rest of the world. The number of cases globally had surpassed 2.5 million and the number in the US had surpassed 800,000, accounting for one-third of all cases worldwide – and over a million by the end of the month; the number of deaths had surpassed 58,000. Shockingly, more Americans had died from COVID-19 than were killed in the Vietnam War. There was an incline in cases in Africa, Central and South America and Eastern Europe in the middle of April and while these countries were at the start of their peak, elsewhere other countries were reaching and passing their peaks. WHO Director, General Tedros Adhanom Ghebreyesus said, "Make no mistake: we have a long way to go. This virus will be with us for a long time." We were preparing for many more months of uncertainty as we were warned that things would not get back to normal any time soon – and, in some cases, may never get back to normal.

Things for Boris Johnson improved when he left hospital on 12th April to continue his recovery at home. He could not praise the National Health Service (NHS) enough as he claimed that they saved his life; in particular, he praised two nurses who looked after him the whole week he was in hospital. There was relief around the nation that he was out of hospital, especially as his fiancée was due to give birth any day, and this had naturally caused worry and fear as she was unable to visit him in hospital. We also learned that Prince Charles had tested positive for COVID-19; however, he had recovered whilst self-isolating at home.

As the WHO continued to work on vaccines, patients were injected with the first human COVID-19 vaccine trial in Europe on 23rd April. Other programmes were set up by the WHO to try and speed up the production of vaccines, but it wasn't a quick process. We were potentially six months in with the virus, so it seems the WHO were not prepared for what was to come – which raised the concerns of Donald Trump. At this time, some countries were looking at 'immunity passports' and started testing those who had developed anti-bodies after they contracted COVID-19, which would allow for more individuals to go back to work sooner and to travel, etc. However, there was no evidence at this stage that someone who'd had the virus could not contract it again, therefore more research was needed.

As we stayed at home and continued to watch the news and adhere to the guidelines, our reality was a little bleak. However, we spent more time sharing moments with our friends and families on video chats and talking to people we hadn't spoken to in a while. I was starting to realise that there were some positives to lockdown – and watching the news every day for long periods of time really wasn't healthy for our minds. As the global death toll surpassed 200,000, compared to 800 deaths with the SARS virus, it was a little difficult to get people to be positive and to think of all the great things around them at this time.

There was more to all this sadness; we just had to look deeper...

Chapter 7
The Good and The Bad

May 2020, and we were now over a month into lockdown in the UK. I was getting used to being at home but I wanted to make the best of this time, as it wasn't something that came around often. I started to notice that lockdown was helping people in many different ways. Having had surgery in February, I found that my body had more time to heal as I wasn't rushing around every day, which was a blessing; I was also able to heal a toenail that was damaged when I hit it against the sharp edge of a door. Now, that doesn't sound so great – and it really wasn't (who likes feet and toes anyway...?) – but being at home meant the air could get to my feet every day, which was amazing, and not having to wear work heels was a nice feeling.

The weather during lockdown was incredible. We may not have been allowed to go out and do anything but we were blessed with glorious sunny weather – which meant more time in the garden, having BBQs, exercising and just relaxing in the comfort of our homes. I witnessed so many people with a lovely tan as they basked outside for weeks, and you would hear people saying, "Who needs to go on holiday when you have amazing weather like this?" That old saying about April showers was certainly not the case in the UK in 2020, and many families were able to enjoy their time together outdoors.

The weather also allowed for a lot of gardening and outdoor projects; I had never mowed my lawn so often in a short space of time. I am absolutely certain that my grass was growing at a faster rate than normal, as if it knew I had plenty of time on my hands. The BBC reported on "seed companies across the UK reporting huge spikes in sales at the beginning of lockdown" and the Royal Horticultural Society (RHS) said it had "seen hundreds of thousands more people use our gardening advice pages compared with last year". Lockdown had allowed for all these great things to happen, in many cases for the first time, or at least for the first time in a long while.

Cooking was something else we invested more time in. Social media was flooded with photos of delicious plates of good food, with recipes being shared between friends and family. Baking was very popular, with 45% of Britons turning to cooking and British grocers seeing a 92% increase in purchases of flour in the four weeks to 22 March, according to the BBC, who continued: "That's an extra 2.1 million people who bought flour in those four weeks compared with the year before." More posts appeared on social media of amazing cakes and pastries, and they all looked divine, which then naturally caused more people to want to appear in their own version of the *Great British Bake Off*!

We found that many families and couples were appreciating their time together. The BBC reported that "More than half of Britons (54%) say spending more time with people in their households has helped them cope, according to the ONS." Sometimes, when we are all rushing around with the many things we have to do in life, we forget to sit down and appreciate family time – and many households were enjoying doing just that. It brought people closer together who would otherwise be busy worrying about the stresses of work, or going out with friends rather than spending time with their family. Many couples in new relationships took the plunge and moved in with each other, otherwise they wouldn't be able to see each other for quite some time, and this also brought couples closer together to learn more about each other.

As we were allowed to go out for an hour every day to do exercise, we saw an increase in people walking, running and cycling. I had the urge to buy a bike – I live in an area with lots of fields and green space and I thought bike rides would be lovely. However, I soon established that the availability of bikes was an issue; every website I checked had sold out of the mid-range models and were left with only very expensive bikes. Justifying the cost of a bike and the frequency I would be cycling didn't make sense, so I put that idea to rest. But it was interesting to see the effect of supply and demand on certain items during lockdown.

Indoors, there was an increase in people watching films and using streaming services as they spent more time at home. The BBC confirmed that "Almost six in ten people (57%) say they are watching films or using streaming services to help ease the impact of the crisis, according to the ONS." It was also reported that "Separate research by Ipsos Mori suggests households are watching more TV overall, with an average of five hours more each week being consumed than before lockdown." It was safe to say the TV was a valuable item in our homes at that time, and one thing that really contributed to keeping many people sane and content during lockdown.

Lockdown brought out people's caring natures. "Community spirit has also grown, ONS data suggests," the BBC reported, "with eight in ten adults (80%) saying they think people are doing more to help others than before the pandemic began." Around the country, we saw people helping those who were vulnerable, by doing weekly shopping for the elderly, for example. There were opportunities to sign up as a volunteer to help the NHS by answering telephone calls, delivering medication and making scrubs and face masks. As a nation, we were pulling together to help out where it was required, and it was great to see.

One of the most important things we witnessed was the increase in socialising virtually. We were not allowed to see our friends and families in person, so what better way than to become a digital social whiz! ONS survey data showed "Almost eight in ten respondents (78%) cite contacting important people in their lives over the phone, social media or video conferencing as a key factor in coping while being at home." This was particularly important for those who were self-isolating for longer periods of time because they were at high risk; communication was key, particularly for their mental health. We saw a huge increase in users of Zoom, which was used for meetings, conferences and family/friend catch ups. Zoom said: "Global daily users went from around 10 million in December last year to a massive 300 million in April 2020." Other apps like Houseparty had an increase in users and of course social media apps like Facebook, Instagram and Snapchat were among the most popular being used.

There was, however, one more communication platform making its mark: TikTok. The world was going TikTok crazy as people created short dance, talent or lip-sync videos on their mobiles and shared them. There were a handful of songs and routines that were popular, and celebrities were taking part as well as millions of people across the globe. It became infectious. Some people really wanted to be TikTok famous and the number of followers and likes they had become a big deal. I gave it a shot with a belly dance routine, and I know many others who created funny and amusing videos. Soon, we were hooked on watching people we didn't know dance, share advice and pull pranks on loved ones. It was addictive but it made lockdown all the better as a great form of entertainment.

Of course, there were other things we got up to, such as DIY projects and learning something new, from languages and online courses to meditation, playing an instrument and much more. My 'something new' was my newfound interest in meditation, which I hadn't really tried before, and writing this book. I guess I never quite understood meditation and what the benefits were, but I found it served me in many ways, from learning how to slow down my breathing to helping me release tension; in turn, this was helping my IBS, which I had suffered with since childhood. Meditation cleared my mind and gave me purpose; it allowed me time to truly be myself and to learn and grow, and this in itself was powerful.

I had never written or even considered writing a book – I think my college assessments were the closest thing I came to writing – but I had a sudden urge to write. With a calling like that, it was difficult not to try, and if it wasn't good enough to be published then at least I would have something to read when I am older to remind myself and my future children of the events that unfolded in 2020 and beyond. I'd have written a book about an unforgettable story in history. Deep down, I knew more would come of this. I'd vowed to try something new, and I wasn't going to give up on it, so this was another great thing that happened during lockdown: an opportunity to write about what changed in our lives in 2020 and publish it for generations to come.

Exercise was something many people vowed to do; on the other hand, many people put on weight as they took comfort in food and alcohol. In many cases, that was due to boredom. The BBC reported a survey that said: "48% of people say they have put on weight during lockdown ... and 29% say they have drunk more alcohol." However, the spike in food and alcohol intake didn't just derive from boredom but because of increased anxiety and stress levels as we entered into a continued time of uncertainty in our lives.

During May we celebrated Mental Health Awareness Week, and it came at a time when a lot of people needed support and were suffering in many different ways. Those individuals who were at high risk had been told to stay at home for 12 weeks and couldn't go out at all, not even for their one hour of exercise. Others were living alone during lockdown and that also had an impact, as they had to spend a lot of time on their own. Whatever the circumstances, stress, anxiety, uncertainty and fear were rife among a lot of people, and this caused these habits of eating, drinking and even smoking to be more common during this time.

Money was a big dilemma. Employees were furloughed by their employers and the British government did an amazing job of supporting workers by paying 80% of wages for those employed. The *Guardian* confirmed that, "Since 20 April, 8.4 million jobs have been furloughed and £15 billion in wages has been claimed under the furlough scheme." The relief this gave to employees and employers was immense, as it allowed employers to keep staff on and reduce or limit redundancies. However, many employers didn't top up the remaining 20% of wages and therefore that shortfall had an impact on many people across the UK.

However, interest rates were slashed from 0.25% to 0.1% in the UK – "The lowest ever in the Bank [of England]'s 325-year history," according to BBC News – mortgage holidays were available for those who really needed them, and there were great offers and rates on credit cards as finances were reviewed during that time. In many cases, people were able to save money as they couldn't spend it in shops, restaurants, cinemas etc., and the money spent on petrol/diesel dropped as we were confined to our homes. The weekly food shop, however, did take a hit as people either stocked up or bought more food.

Sadly, lockdown affected many relationships and there was an increase in reported domestic violence. BBC News reported that: "It's thought cases have increased by 20% during lockdown, as many people are trapped at home with their abuser." This was horrible to read, especially at a time when having people around you and maintaining a positive mindset was important. There was an increase in online posts and adverts directed at those who were potentially at risk or were already a victim of domestic abuse, asking them to speak up and call a domestic abuse support line for help.

Enquiries into divorce went up significantly during lockdown. Hewitts Solicitors confirmed, "Divorce enquiries have increased by 42% since the commencement of the lockdown in comparison to the same period in 2019." The increase was due to couples spending more time with each other under one roof combined with the added stress and worry over job security, financial concerns and the pressure of home schooling, for those with children. This may have come at a time when couples' relationships were already strained; lockdown simply added to that.

Not only did we see new trends and changes in people and our homes, but the impact lockdown had on the environment was significant. We witnessed clear skies as pollution started to disappear, which improved air quality. The *Guardian* reported a study had revealed: "The improvement in air quality over the past month of the Coronavirus lockdown has led to 11,000 fewer deaths from pollution in the UK and elsewhere in Europe." There were also sharp falls in road traffic and emissions, which impacted on children developing asthma and people struggling to breathe.

Venice was a focal point: their waters were now clear and blue, free of pollution from boats and cruise ships. With a halt on air travel, this also cleared pollution in our skies, which could be seen worldwide. We also witnessed wild animals on the streets of deserted towns.

Many businesses and world leaders have had the battle for sustainability at the forefront of their thoughts for years and it really was amazing to see our world become green again. The question was, is this only temporary? What happens when things get back to normal? Will things ever be normal again? Will our previous life return with the same results and expectations?

As we witnessed so many beautiful things, this was a time of learning. While the death toll was rising globally, we had to think about all the great things the pandemic taught us and think about whether this would change when we were back on the move again. I reflected on this a lot and was optimistic about the future world; at the same time, I had a level of uncertainty about issues such as work, which, in hospitality, wasn't going to pick up immediately. One thing I found helpful was to be grateful for all I had at this time: the roof over my head, the food on my plate, the amazing friends and family I had around me, the job I loved and the little things, like having ears to hear, eyes to see, and legs and arms to express myself with music and dance.

In all that was bad there was a light, and that light was what we had to concentrate on for the future and whatever it looked like. We had countless blessings every day.

It was certainly a challenging time for many, and in

different ways; lockdown may have been good for some and not so great for others. We were still dealing with the unknown and, as we waited for lockdown measures to be eased, there was also the uncertainty of whether things would ever be the same again. In some ways, did we want it to ever be the same again...?

Chapter 8
The Ongoing Picture

Things continued to change around the world as COVID-19 made its way from country to country. On 4th May, world leaders raised 7.4 billion euros to fund the research and distribution of COVID-19 diagnostics, treatments and vaccines. An interesting study in male patients in a hospital in China found that the virus was present in their semen, which was not something that had previously been looked into.

As studies and funding increased to analyse the virus and find vaccines, the World Health Organization confirmed that "although it has seemed like an incredibly long time, we are at the very, very early stages of our understanding of how this virus affects the body, how the disease progresses, what diseases this infection causes". It was evident that we were still a long way away from really understanding the virus that had accounted for more than 4 million cases globally by 9th May.

On 10th May, the Chinese government reported its first new case in Wuhan, where the pandemic originated. It was thought this was due to the government's response in lifting lockdown measures. The WHO had warned against lifting lockdowns prematurely, especially if the right public health surveillance was not in place. But this situation allowed nations across the world to see what was happening in those countries who were ahead in the progress of the virus, such as China and Italy.

Talking of Italy, the lockdown was heavily policed but

finally, after 23 weeks of home confinement and no allowance for outdoor exercise, there was an easing of restrictions. Bars and restaurants reopened on 18 May, but with reduced numbers and social distancing in place. Hairdressers also opened on the same day, as well as mass for those who wanted to go to church. Gyms and swimming pools opened a week later, except in Lombardy, the epicentre of the virus. Further easing of the lockdown was being drawn up for June, including the opening of theatres, cinemas and tourist sites, and the restart of Serie A football, with clubs following later in July. It was a similar story in other European countries, where restrictions slowly eased throughout May; however, in some countries schools were still affected as most children were now commencing in September for the new school year; in some cases, younger children were permitted to go back to school earlier.

On 14th May, the number of deaths from COVID-19 surpassed 300,000 globally and this was continuing to rise. There was a significant increase in cases in Brazil, which was rising higher on the ladder; the United States was at the top with the highest number of cases globally. There was still animosity over the handling of COVID-19 by the WHO and this resulted in 100 countries backing a draft resolution to the World Health Assembly calling for "an independent inquiry into the handling of the Coronavirus crisis, including an impartial comprehensive evaluation into the actions of WHO and their timelines pertaining to the COVID-19 pandemic". It seemed it was not only the US president, Donald Trump, who had questioned the WHO. He later threatened to extend his temporary funding freeze to the WHO permanently.

Trump made more headline news when he confirmed that he had been taking hydroxychloroquine for over a week. The US Food & Drug Administration spoke out against it unproven use and warned him of harmful side effects. Donald Trump certainly raised many eyebrows with his claim, and we soon saw funny social media memes about his unproven belief in this drug. It was later proven that a study of hydroxychloroquine among hospital patients with COVID-19 was linked to increased rates of death. The WHO later put a temporary pause on trials of the use of hydroxychloroquine as a potential treatment for COVID-19.

The rate of cases saw its biggest reporting of COVID-19 on 20th May, when the WHO received confirmation of 106,000 cases in one day. This was the most the agency had seen in a single day since the outbreak began. Globally, there had now been over 6 million cases.

On 5th June, the WHO updated its guidance with regards to the use of masks for those working in clinical areas. Masks had to be worn by all people in these areas and not just those who were looking after patients. Those who were over 60 years old and those with underlying health conditions should also wear masks where social distancing was not possible. Further guidance was issued to governments to ask people to wear masks on public transport and in shops, again where social distancing was difficult. This came after a project confirmed that nearly 600 front-line health workers had died from COVID-19 in the United States. It is evident that those within clinical areas were most at risk of contracting the virus and this could also be seen in the UK, where nurses had sadly lost their lives.

By 8th June, the number of cases globally had surpassed 7 million and the death toll surpassed 400,000. We were not seeing any downturn in cases, although the picture varied across the world, with many countries in the early stages of the virus, others reaching their peak and countries like

Italy now easing lockdown and starting to get things moving again.

Back in the UK, we were over two months into our lockdown and things were starting to feel hopeful as we began to hear of some easing of the rules. June is a month that sees me celebrate my birthday, as well as my mum's and my auntie's in Canada – but this year was a very different year. We were allowed to meet up to six people in the garden as long as we were socially distancing, so on 6th June we celebrated my mum's 60th birthday in the garden with a party of six… a huge difference to the party of 100 that we had planned. It was a big year for my mum, as she wanted to combine her 60th birthday with a charity fundraiser for the Macmillan charity after having cancer in 2018/2019. Because she had diabetes and was in remission from cancer, she was one of the millions of people who received a letter from the government saying they must stay at home for 12 weeks as the effects of COVID-19 could be worse for them – but her birthday was the one day I really wanted to give her a hug, after not being able to for months…

I was inspired by a story I saw in the news that showed two people hugging, wearing full PPE, masks and plastic coverings to separate them – and I thought maybe I could do the same. I purchased two masks where the funds would go to charity and, after a clear out, I found a poncho from a trip to Universal Studios many years ago. I didn't say anything to my mum. Off I went to her garden gathering and the anticipated words from her mouth when I got there were: "It's my 60th birthday and I really want to give you a hug!"

"I had a great idea…" I said, and off I went to get our masks and poncho. My mum was laughing as I appeared in this big poncho for those wet days at a theme park. I handed over her mask and we embraced. What a great feeling it was to hug my mum after so long – and especially on her 60th birthday – whilst maintaining a degree of safety with my version of PPE. And I have a lovely photo we can look back on in years to come to show how life changed in 2020 and how much we missed the little things in life, like giving and receiving hugs.

It may not have been the amazing bash she wanted, but it was a lovely day all the same, with immediate family celebrating my mum's big birthday. It really was a time for appreciating the little things in life.

The next celebration was a week later when we celebrated my birthday. Again, the same rules applied with social distancing and meeting in the garden. We enjoyed great food and drink, and I had my favourite Italian cream birthday cake as a surprise, which was absolutely amazing! Having been keto for several months, it was worth having a day off just to eat a delicious slice of fresh cream cake with fresh fruit on top and crushed hazelnuts around the side. As we embraced our new normal for however long it would last, another great lockdown birthday was had, and more great memories were made to look back on in the years to come.

It was welcome news on 15th June when lockdown restrictions started to ease. Non-essential shops could reopen as long as they adhered to social distancing rules, and we saw early-morning queues for Primark in London as people were eager to get back into the shops after many months – although many people had shopped online instead. *Internet Retailing* confirmed that: "60% of UK consumers admit to purchasing more during lockdown," which was expected, as we spent more time online. I definitely noticed that I ordered more online: I saw adverts for items I thought were cool, and I was soon tempted by the online splurge.

We also welcomed the opening of zoos and safari parks, as long as food items were takeaway only in the cafes. Secondary schools started to reopen, with social distancing measures in place, as well as churches and other places of worship. It was great to see shops reopen and the empty car parks filled with cars again, and to see people start to lead a sub-normal life.

Public transport was a key area, with advice being to avoid public transport if possible and use cars or bikes to get around. The wearing of masks was also mandatory on all forms of public transport. I took a trip to London for an appointment and measures were in place to ensure people adhered to the rules, such as reminders when purchasing tickets and announcements at the stations that masks must be worn. There was, however, no policing of this, and I witnessed a handful of people who were not wearing masks on the train, which demonstrated who took it seriously and who didn't.

Elsewhere in the world, China reported on 14th June that they had 57 new cases of COVID-19 and Beijing shut its largest fruit and vegetable market following positive tests of 45 people who had visited. This was after 50 days without a case being reported in the capital. The fact that more cases of COVID-19 had derived from a Chinese market was cause for concern, and we watched for further developments.

In June, more than 100,000 new cases were reported almost every day in a two-week period. General Tedros Adhanom Ghebreyesus of WHO was quoted as saying: "Nearly 75% of these new cases have come from 20 countries, which are mostly in the Americas and South Asia." By the middle of June, the confirmed number of COVID-19 cases had surpassed 8 million globally. There seemed to be no end in sight, as cases continued to be confirmed and more trials were being completed to find a vaccine for the virus. Seven months on from the initial reported cases in China, we were still battling with the virus and nowhere near to having a vaccine that could potentially save millions of lives.

However, on 16th June, results were published of a clinical trial of a steroid called dexamethasone, which could reduce mortality by about one third in COVID-19 patients on ventilators. It is said that this was the first drug shown to save the lives of people requiring oxygen or ventilator support, and it was affordable in most countries, according to the WHO.

Following trials of the drug, Donald Trump boasted that he was taking it as a way to protect himself from catching the virus. The WHO had now confirmed it was dropping hydroxychloroquine as a potential treatment as its use did not result in a reduction in the mortality of hospitalized COVID-19 patients.

On 18th June, a study published in *Nature Medicine* found that the levels of antibodies in patients who had recovered from COVID-19 had declined significantly two to three months after infection. This raised questions about how long people were immune to contracting the virus again. There were still many trials taking place and governments were working hard to keep nations safe as well as investing in research that could change the course of action across the world.

The WHO's General Ghebreyesus said that we were "in a new dangerous phase, as many people are tired of staying home and governments are eager to reopen their economies, but the virus is spreading fast and most people globally are still susceptible to contracting it". The clinical trial of the steroid dexamethasone had shown some potential in saving lives of critically ill COVID-19 patients; however, the next stage would be to look at increasing production and distribution of the drug, ensuring it was inexpensive and manufactured globally.

Towards the end of June, the WHO outlined details on contact tracing: a method of controlling the outbreak by governments notifying individuals who had been in contact with someone diagnosed with the virus and advising them of what to do if they became unwell. Many countries argued that they felt this would be too difficult to do, as there were so many cases. The WHO suggested that if any country believed contact tracing was difficult then it was a "lame excuse". They also confirmed that they were planning on sending a team to China to investigate the origins of COVID-19.

The UK was ahead of the game, having started their Test and Trace system on 28th May. The rules were that if anyone had been in contact with someone with COVID-19, they would have to stay at home and self-isolate for 14 days. They would not be able to leave the house for any reason: food and medicine would need to be ordered online, they could not have any visitors and they had to isolate from those they lived with.

If at any point someone developed symptoms then they would need to get a test done as soon as possible to check if they had COVID-19, and anyone living with them or in their 'support bubble' would need to self-isolate while they waited on results. The support bubble was for people living alone, allowing them to meet one other household.

If the results were positive, the individual would need to share information as soon as possible on their recent contacts to the NHS Test and Trace service to help alert others who may need to self-isolate.

At this point, we did not know how successful the system was as there was a degree of trust that was required by the British public to report in a prompt and accurate manner; however, we would hopefully know more over the coming months.

An interesting article was published in *Tuko* on 21st June, quoting an Italian professor, Matteo Bassetti, who claimed that the virus was weakening by itself, a vaccine was no longer necessary to quell it, and although it wasn't scientifically proven, there was a huge likelihood that COVID-19 was mutating and losing its virulence. It was an interesting read, as Bassetti explained that in March and April there was difficulty managing the illness and now the virus was likely to be mutating, with fewer people requiring oxygen and ventilation.

This came at the same time as the WHO stated that the virus was spreading fast. Therefore, with no scientific evidence of Bassetti's claims, the world was still treating the virus with the highest concern as we reached six months since the first reported case in China.

Chapter 9
Four Months Into Lockdown

July 2020, and confirmed cases of COVID-19 surpassed 11 million globally, only five days after they hit 10 million.

On 6th July, the US submitted formal notification to withdraw from the WHO, after several threats from Donald Trump over the last few months. It was now being reviewed to see whether the US had met the conditions to do so. At the same time, 239 scientists urged the WHO to "recognise the potential for an airborne spread of COVID-19" as most public health organisations did not currently do so.

Brazil, which was just behind the US with the second highest number of cases at 1.7 million, confirmed that President Jair Bolsonaro had tested positive for COVID-19 after downplaying the virus for several months. Bolsonaro said he was taking hydroxychloroquine, which he claimed had been proven to treat COVID-19; at the same time, he had criticized public health measures and quarantine rules. This just showed that no one was immune to the virus. As for leaders such as Bolsonaro, the public felt he needed to be doing more to support his country and his people through this pandemic rather than criticizing public health organisations.

Elsewhere in the world, confirmed cases of COVID-19 had surpassed 500,000 in Africa, with cases doubling in the space of a month in some countries including Egypt, Algeria, Nigeria and South Africa. By 8th July, cases globally had surpassed 12 million, a rise of 1 million in just

5 days, which was unbelievable.

Restrictions differed in countries across the globe. Sadly my aunt, who lived in Canada, had been diagnosed with stage 4 cancer and we really wanted to be there with her; however, due to restrictions at the Canadian borders we were unable to visit, which was very sad for our family. I can imagine that these restrictions impacted many families as more and more people were confirmed to have COVID-19 and, sadly, many lost their lives with no family around them. It was a very tough time. Not only did the pandemic affect people's mental health, it also prevented families from seeing each other and being together when they most needed it.

A UK study had analysed 90 patients and health care workers and found that only 17% of them retained an antibody response to COVID-19 three months later. This was interesting to read; however, it also demonstrated that a second wave of the virus could potentially impact individuals again, as they may have weak antibodies.

On 13th July, the *2020 State of Food Security and Nutrition in the World* report estimated that "between 83 million and 1,132 million people could be pushed into hunger due to COVID-19 as many people lose their jobs". The furlough scheme in the UK had been amazing, but many companies were now reviewing structures and headcount before changes to the scheme came into effect in August. To date, the government had been paying 80% of people's wages and in some cases companies were unable to top up the remaining 20%, so households were running at a loss. As of August 2020, companies in the UK had to start paying national insurance and pension contributions; therefore July was a month of despair for many employees as they heard their employers were going to be making redundancies.

Some of the largest companies affected by redundancies were:

- British Petroleum – 10,000 jobs
- Centrica – 5,000 jobs
- Rolls Royce – 9,000 jobs
- Pret A Manger – 30 shops
- Mulberry – 25% of their workforce
- Bella Italia, Café Rouge, Las Iguanas – 1,900 jobs
- British Airways – up to 12,000 jobs
- easyJet – 4,500 jobs
- Virgin Atlantic – 3,000 jobs
- Boots – 4,000 jobs
- John Lewis – 1,300 jobs
- Ryanair – 3,000 jobs
- Renault – 15,000 jobs
- Airbus – 15,000 jobs
- TUI – 8,000 jobs

These were major players in the market, and there were also many smaller businesses that had to close their doors because of COVID-19. Euronews reported that "281,000 people in the European Union lost their jobs in June, which came after the number of people unemployed rose by 253,000 in May and 397,000 in April." It was looking dire for many organisations as they tried to manage the pandemic, and this resulted in many job losses, with some businesses unfortunately unable to survive. Some big names went into administration, some of which were bought out, including:

- Benson for Beds
- Harvey's Furniture
- Cath Kidson
- TM Lewin
- Monsoon
- Victoria's Secret
- Aldo
- Debenhams

2020 was proving to be the worst year ever for many businesses, Britain's economy plunged into a recession the likes of which it hadn't seen for 300 years, according to the *Guardian*. The hardest hit industries were wholesale, retail, accommodation and food sectors, although supermarkets were not impacted as much because of the need for people to continue to buy food. However, supermarkets had been affected in a different way during the early days of lockdown because of the sheer demand and increase in home deliveries.

The impact on households was also significant. Sky News reported that the "Coronavirus crisis delivered the biggest income shock since the mid-1970s as typical earnings immediately plunged by 4.5% from the run up to lockdown to May". The government schemes had been instrumental in keeping people in jobs; however, as we had seen, alongside the phasing out of the Job Retention Scheme and the withdrawal of Universal Credit increases for 2021, it was certain that this would continue to impact households and businesses for many months to come.

From July, the economy slowly began to open up. We saw

more people in restaurants and there was a general feeling of things starting to look up – although normal was nowhere near, as we continued to adopt new practices in line with government rules.

Hairdressers were allowed to open again across the UK on 5th July, and I was excited. We'd seen many lockdown hairstyles, from long hair with split ends and outgrowing roots to men also enduring long hair and big beards. As a nation, we were desperate to get to the hairdresser or barber for that long-awaited haircut, so much so that it was exciting news to be telling others you had an appointment. Prior to my hairdresser appointment, I received information on what to expect when I arrived and what I would have to wear. Upon entering, I had my temperature checked and I had to wear a mask throughout; all the hairdressers also wore masks and visors and each section was divided off, so social distancing measures were in place. For someone like me with long hair, having a colour and cut could take up to three hours, therefore by the end of my appointment I felt like I had given myself a nice facial from the warmth of my breath under my mask! I wouldn't say it was the most joyful of experiences, though, and I was soon pulling my mask off and breathing in the outdoor air with such relief.

It was at this moment that I remembered how much we potentially didn't appreciate in life. Pre- COVID-19 life was normal and good for many – and now we had to adapt to our new normal and learn to appreciate different things. It felt great to have luscious locks again – I felt I could appear in my own version of an L'Oreal advert and say: "Because I am worth it."

That was just one moment that brought some joy as we were slowly released from three months of lockdown. Another came on 18th July, when I was very happy to be able to get my nails done again. For those of us who like to pamper ourselves every once in a while, this was another great experience. Although face masks were again mandatory, I was also given my own file and buffer set, which I would have to bring in with me every time to avoid cross contamination. It was strange at first, but we were starting to accept that this was how it had to be and it could last some time, so we had to embrace it.

On 24th July we saw new rules come into effect with regards to face coverings having to be worn in most public spaces, including all shops, supermarkets, shopping centres, banks and cinemas. There were fines in place for those failing to do so – £100, or £50 if paid within 14 days – and this would be enforced by the police rather than shop workers.

It is safe to say that most of the British public did follow the rules and we were soon seeing a vast array of face masks, from the simplest to colourful ones to outright funny ones that showed off their wearers' character and humour. The face mask was one of those very important things you needed to always have on you in addition to your purse/wallet, phone and keys. I resorted to buying a face mask case – yes, they did exist! I shared my thoughts on this new necessity with friends, because who wants to put a mask on when it's been thrown in a handbag or left on the side, so you're inhaling a load of rubbish? I pitched my idea on it to several people and it hadn't crossed their minds, but 'Miss Paranoid' over here was ahead of it all.

There were moments when I would think about everything and it still felt surreal that we were experiencing this – and not only in the UK, but worldwide. With everyone having a common goal of preventing the virus from spreading, you did see nearly everyone in the shops wearing masks, and it dawned on me that this wasn't just anything; this was something that was impacting so many lives in different ways. To think that I had more time off in 2020 than I worked is unbelievable; however, it wouldn't have been possible to write this book without having this time off, and one day in many years to come I will be reading this again as a reminder of it being the strangest year of our lives.

Many bizarre things cropped up in the news during 2020. One interesting article stated that working from home meant more money was spent on tea and biscuits. That probably isn't as exciting as it sounds, but I felt inclined to read about it. Sky News said that "British shoppers are spending millions more on tea, coffee and biscuits, with the cost of working from home starting to add up." Now here is the interesting bit: data from Kantar showed that in the four weeks to 12th July, "£24 million was spent on tea and coffee and £19 million more on biscuits compared to the same period last year". What a huge increase in costs, as the British public made sure they had enough stock of their favourite tea, coffee and biscuits to keep them going whilst working from home.

July was a month in which people started to get back to work because of the easing of lockdown measures. However, many people were still homebound and on furlough as businesses across the UK were still not busy enough to have the majority of their staff back. July was a significant month as we welcomed the following easing of restrictions:

- Gyms, fitness centres, dance studios and swimming pools were open
- Wedding receptions were permitted for up to 30 people
- Performances with live audiences could commence if

pilots were successful

- Bowling alleys, skating rinks, theme parks and cinemas could open with social distancing in place
- Tattooists, spas and tanning salons could open with some restrictions
- Pubs and restaurants were open
- Hair salons and barbers opened their doors
- Shops opened
- Property viewings recommenced
- You could go on holiday in self-contained accommodation
- Years 1 and 6 were able to return to school
- Gatherings in groups of six people in public or private outdoor spaces whilst social distancing were allowed

It was a much-awaited time for the country as we were finally 'allowed' to go out and eat in restaurants, visit friends and family and see life come back to our streets, towns and cities. As I looked back on lockdown, I still couldn't believe what we had experienced and how drastically life had changed.

Four months on from the start of lockdown and things were far from normal, as we continued to wear masks in most public places and there was still about jobs, how long this would go on for, and also the worry of a second outbreak in the winter. 2020 was proving to be a very weird and surreal year.

Chapter 10
Summertime!

As life started to move again in July and travel restrictions were slowly easing, this meant many people were considering travelling or going on 'staycations' in the UK. However, things still looked dreary as cases continued to rise, with cases surpassing 13 million globally. Ever-challenging medical trials continued around the world in countries eager to develop a successful vaccine.

A programme called COVAX (COVID-19 Vaccine Global Access) was introduced whereby countries joined to gain increasing equitable access to future COVID-19 vaccines, which would be financed by individual countries through their budgets. This would mean that when a suitable vaccine was found, investment to manufacture it would be available to achieve significant volumes. By 15th July, there were already 75 countries who had expressed an interest in the programme.

As further tests were carried out, some studies found that fragments of coronavirus were found in the stools of COVID-19 patients, and more research was being done into the possibility of oral-faecal transmission of COVID-19. This, however, had not yet been demonstrated. On 17th July, confirmed cases surpassed 14 million and confirmed deaths surpassed 600,000 globally. Also on this day, the UK secured advance access to 90 million doses of three promising vaccines.

On 3rd August, Chinese and WHO experts drafted plans for an investigation into the origins of COVID-19, which was going to begin in Wuhan. The aim was to identify the links between cases and identify when the virus crossed from animals to humans, paving the way to a better understanding of its source. There were estimates that the fatality rate of COVID-19 was 0.6%; however, as low as this sounds, it was quite high according to Maria van Kerkhove of the WHO.

The relationship between the US and the WHO was still a sore subject; as the Director General of the WHO said, "Money is not the issue; it's actually the relationship with the US which is more important, and its leadership role." The reports continued to be blurred as there appeared to be more behind the reasons for the US removing its funding; it seemed like something was being kept under wraps – and more was to come of it in time.

By 10th August, confirmed cases of COVID-19 hit 20 million, with cases in the US surpassing 5 million, the African continent surpassing 1 million – and New Zealand reporting 100 days of no community transmission. The message from WHO Director General Tedros Adhanom Ghebreyesus was to "suppress, suppress, suppress the virus ... Behind these statistics is a great deal of pain and suffering ... There are green shoots of hope and no matter where a country, a region, a city or a town is – it's never too late to turn the outbreak around."

The figures were saying otherwise, as confirmed cases increased significantly, in some cases by a million in less than a week. In Brazil, second after the US, the virus was continuing to spread by 50,000 to 60,000 cases a day. Brazil's president Jair Bolsonaro was continuing to tout the drug hydroxychloroquine and how it could fight the disease; however, it was being communicated that the drug wasn't in fact a proven effective treatment.

Coming back to the situation in the UK, holidays abroad

were questionable because of the dreaded quarantine rules for certain countries, lack of information about whether we would go into another lockdown and the risk of not being able to get back home if we did. With so many businesses going into administration, the reduced demand in travel and concern about what to expect on arrival in other countries meant it was a safer bet to remain in the UK.

Many people spent the time at home, enjoying the glorious weather we had at the time. I had never seen so much sunshine as we did whilst in lockdown. It certainly helped us get through the worst of it.

It is interesting how time can determine a lot of what we do in life. We are forever saying "There is not enough time in the day" or "I just don't have time", but in 2020 we were at a point where many of us could say we had so much time to do things, we didn't know what to do when we had nothing left to do! Luckily, things were picking up and there was movement again. It was so refreshing to see this, but for how long would it last? There were already rumours of a second national lockdown…

On 3rd August, the UK government launched the 'Eat Out to Help Out' initiative, giving us all 50% off food in participating restaurants every Monday to Wednesday in August. This was put in place to help protect jobs within the hospitality industry, which had been massively impacted by the pandemic. The scheme certainly helped get people out: we were like birds wanting to fly again after having our wings clipped! What we saw was a huge demand in people wanting to eat out – and why not, with 50% off?

However, the challenge was most of these restaurants had had to make redundancies and didn't now have the staff to manage the service levels that were required. It was a great initiative but businesses struggled to keep up with the demand. In many cases, Thursdays to Sundays saw the complete opposite, with quiet restaurants and staff who were tired after a manic three days. It certainly was a time of fear and the unknown, with a mix of hope and faith that things would move to a better place in time.

In August we also saw a march for fair pay for NHS workers in the UK, as they were at the forefront of the battle with COVID. The NHS were working day in and day out to help people survive a virus that they had never experienced before, one that was so deadly, one that put their own lives at risk. I couldn't wear my mask for long periods of time and couldn't imagine what it was like for nurses and doctors who had to wear a mask for eight hours or more a day, working in critical environments for months. An article in the *Guardian* stated that "if we really want an NHS capable of dealing with a crisis and all the other demands, then the government must start treating health care workers with dignity and respect and this starts with fair pay". The same article confirmed that "a recent survey by the Royal College of Nursing of 42,000 nursing staff showed that 36% were considering leaving the profession, with most citing pay as a factor". It was such a tough time for the NHS, but the nation was behind them all the way and they were seen as superheroes for all they were doing.

With the UK coming out of lockdown, many companies had to look at projected business and demand in a month that saw little light at the end of a long tunnel. It was reported by the British Foreign Policy Group that "nearly 1,800 companies in the UK planned to cut 20 or more jobs" and data showed that "the number of employed people in the UK fell by 730,000 between March and July". The impact the pandemic was having on business was horrific, and the fear that this also caused amongst individuals was immense. Key questions to be asked included: How does a nation bounce back from this? What is the government doing to support people and business? How long do we anticipate this going on for? The sad truth was, it was all an unknown. We had to ride the wave of uncertainty and simply hope that our jobs were safe, our bodies and minds were healthy, and we didn't take any of what we had for granted.

One thing that was evident, confirmed by the British Foreign Policy Group (BFPG), was that "figures showed depression among British adults doubled during the pandemic". Everything that was going on in the UK and the world was enough to push people into a really bad place, mentally; it took a lot to be resilient in a world that was becoming a nightmare for many.

Towards the end of August, the BFPG confirmed that the global death toll had reached 800,000 as cases passed 25 million. With no sign of the virus going away anytime soon, still more COVID vaccine testing was taking place in China as well as Russia and Australia; the fear was a vaccine would be rolled out without passing conventional testing phases.

August was a tough month for me and my family as my auntie in Canada, who had been diagnosed with cancer, lost her battle. With much of the attention going to COVID patients, it was a tough time for my family to be with my aunt whilst she was in hospital. I recall my cousin being in a full protection suit, and only one person could visit at a time. The worst part was that we couldn't be there, as the Canadian government had placed a ban on travel into Canada except for residents or visits to immediate family, which didn't include aunties or even sisters – so not even my mum could head out there.

It was awful having to say goodbye on a FaceTime call. We still couldn't travel even after my aunt's passing to go to her funeral. Watching videos of the service and trying to support family from afar was the best we could do under the circumstances. Many people lost loved ones during this time, some to COVID and some to other causes, but the saddest part was how many people died alone because family were not allowed to be by their side. It was tragic, and it really did put so much into perspective about being grateful for our loved ones and appreciating every minute of every day, because we don't know when it is our last. August was a month that changed so much for me and I had to be strong for my mum and many other people who needed my positive energy and compassion.

Whilst I was on furlough, I really wanted to make the best use of my time before going back to work. I had many people want to speak to me about their jobs and, with my experience in HR, I was able to guide them. People also spoke to me about their relationship with their partners, as it was a tough time managing everything.

As I am a Mental Health First Aider, I also had a number of people who just wanted to get my perspective on things, and one comment in one of these conversations changed everything for me. A friend said to me, "You should be a coach with everything you are doing." For a moment, I thought, *Nooo, this is only temporary,* but the more I thought about it, the more it sank in that I should be a life coach. Normally when I get an idea in my head I tend to run with it, and this was one of those times. I realised I had the time to do this, it was something I could do alongside work, and I could also support my coaching within the workplace – so why not?

In a blink of an eye, I was googling coaching courses and trying to find the right programme for me. This gave me such joy. It was something I could really look forward to, and it got my brain working again after several months of not engaging on a more stimulating level. I was embarking on a new journey, one that felt right for me as I wanted to help people and inspire their growth. I was so excited to get started. In the midst of a global crisis, my story as a life coach was now starting to unfold.

Chapter 11
The Conspiracies Begin

By September, a number of conspiracies had emerged that were making some people question what was going on; others didn't want to entertain the conspiracies, as they believed what they were told on the news. A tremendous fear engulfed us: we feared for our lives, our health, the health of loved ones, our jobs, our relationships – but there was also a fear of the information we were being given. This led to some people downplaying the virus and ignoring public health advice on the grounds that we were potentially being given misleading information.

Some people were strongly against the rules had been put in place by governments worldwide. Some of these rules were seen to be going against our human rights and many questioned how we could possibly be in this situation. *Scientific American* published some of the conspiracy theories, including the following:

1. Coronavirus was engineered in a lab in China. As the virus had emerged from Wuhan, China, there were theories that it started in a lab there, and further speculation that it was engineered as a bioweapon. There was no solid evidence to suggest this was the case and further investigation was required to determine the credibility of this theory.

2. Wealthy elites internationally spread the virus to win power and profit. In a conspiracy theory video called *Plandemic,* a woman named Judy Mikovits made claims that Microsoft co-founder Bill Gates had used his power to profit from the disease. The video was shared by anti-vaxxers and generated more than eight million views on YouTube and Facebook, amongst other channels. It was later taken down because of its misinformation.

3. COVID-19 is no worse than the flu. There were a lot of claims that the virus was just like any other flu that we would have annually; however, information was provided that deaths caused by COVID were significantly higher than those of seasonal flu.

4. The vaccine will be unsafe and a bigger risk than getting COVID-19. Many people said they would not get a vaccine once it was available, as there were claims that it would kill people and cause other illnesses to emerge. The race was underway to make a vaccine; however, many anti-vaxxers claimed it takes years to develop a vaccine and questioned how it was now possible to achieve this in several months.

Many conspiracy theories emerged early in the pandemic, with more developing as time went by. At this point we didn't know what would be in a vaccine, how it would impact us or how it would be mandated to try and combat the virus. It was the idea that it was being rolled out globally that really made people question what was going on. To have governments across the world embark on the same journey and implement similar rulings made some people feel like there was a much bigger 'operation' going on that we knew nothing about.

Furthermore, the Chinese doctor who raised the alarm about coronavirus in the very early days of the outbreak was alleged to have died after catching the virus from a patient. An article on BBC News claimed that Dr Li tried to send a message to fellow medics about the outbreak at the end of December, and three days later the police visited him to tell him to stop. He was said to have been spreading rumours and was later summoned to the Public Security Bureau, where he was told to sign a letter accusing him of "making false comments" that had "severely disturbed the social order". He published a letter about what happened and, later, received an apology from local authorities but it was too late; the virus had started to spread, becoming an emergency on 20th January.

There were theories that Dr Li knew what was coming and was trying to warn medics, but he faced obstruction and had to sign agreements confirming that what he was saying was 'false comments' because the authorities didn't want people to know. It was claimed that it was all planned and created for a bigger purpose. Dr Li was in hospital for some time but later died of the virus; however, he was hailed a hero for identifying the virus and trying to spread awareness of its danger to others.

It was becoming apparent that many anti-vaxxers were starting to raise awareness of what they thought could possibly be going on and what was to come, with videos being shared on non-official online channels and forwarded via messaging apps.

I remember seeing videos of imminent lockdowns before anything was officially announced, and others encouraging us to ensure we had enough food and resources. Ultimately, this created a sense of panic and people flocked to the shops to try and buy more than they needed just in case we had another lockdown, resulting in item restrictions to ensure everyone could get a share of the limited food items.

As we headed into autumn things started to change, with further restrictions coming into force. With Christmas looming, people started to wonder what was going to happen and questioned whether or not they would be able to have a Christmas with their loved ones.

Chapter 12
The Autumn Blues

As September 2020 arrived, there were some developments across the globe as many countries declared their state of affairs. Earlier I mentioned COVAX, which was the international effort to create and distribute a vaccine; the US had refused to join the programme, stating they were not interested in the effort as it was organised by the WHO.

At this time, the WHO also confirmed that a widespread vaccine would not be possible until mid-2021, so until then we would have to sustain measures to limit the spread of the virus. As various conspiracy theories circulated, it appeared there was hesitancy in some countries to be vaccinated, with 44% of Greeks claiming they would refuse the vaccine. In Croatia, thousands joined a 'Covidiot' rally against coronavirus measures. The situation was very different in Brazil, where only 5% of people said they would refuse the vaccine.

Cases continued to increase, with more than 27 million cases globally and India becoming the country with the second highest number of infections. There seemed to be no easing in the number of cases being recorded each day. It was all we were hearing on the news and there was concern that another lockdown was imminent if things did not improve going into winter.

On 14th September, over fears of a second wave, the UK government introduced the 'rule of six', which banned gatherings of more than six people indoors and outdoors.

This resulted in many cancelled plans with friends and family and limited events like birthday celebrations and parties, making many people feel sad that they couldn't go about their normal activities. Documents were also leaked suggesting the government were pinning their hopes on an initiative named Operation Moonshot, a £100 billion mass testing programme, to avoid a second lockdown.

In addition, there seemed to be a mismatch in information coming out, as the WHO was confirming that vaccines would be available in mid-2021 and the UK government was claiming vaccinations would avoid another lockdown – but rumours were spreading that another one was imminent, well ahead of the 2021 vaccination rollout, so how could this be possible?

Facebook stated at this time that they would not remove anti-vaccine posts, which were increasing in number, and this led to people reading more and more about what we should be thinking versus what we were being told by the mainstream media. Anti-lockdown protestors clashed with other protestors in London, causing disruption in the capital.

The WHO predicted that Europe would see a rise in coronavirus cases in October and November, and particularly as we went into winter, which is when a lot of people would naturally have seasonal flu. On 17th September, they warned of "alarming rates of transmission" across Europe, and France declared it had hit a new record of over 13,000 daily cases.

We were waiting to hear about another lockdown whilst trying to live a seemingly normal life. We didn't want restrictions to put us back in a place where life was limited. However, just as many people started to get back into work and find their feet again, further restrictions were imposed upon us. Doctors in the UK were urging for tighter restrictions and, on 22nd September, the Prime Minister brought back a return to home working and a 10pm curfew for the hospitality sector.

This meant we could continue going out and eating out – but not past 10pm. Hospitality venues closed their doors early to abide by the new rulings and halt the rise in cases. Weddings were also affected by the restrictions and could only be held with 15 people. Although most people wanted to go out and enjoy a 'normal life', these restrictions made some people feel they did not want to go out. And people were still worried about their own jobs, whether their employers would survive the pandemic, not having enough money living on while furloughed, not being able to afford to go out and eat. It was a tough time for millions of people who wanted normality: we had little bits of it, but the reality was that life was very different and this resulted in many staying indoors.

Further talks happened about a vaccine, with President Trump saying he expected to have enough vaccines for every American by April 2021. A total of 156 countries had agreed to the COVID vaccine allocation deal to ensure equitable access and we were hearing more and more about this possible vaccine; however, it seemed it would take some time to get to us.

Events across the globe were either being cancelled or going ahead with limitations. Rio de Janeiro's carnival was postponed for the first time in a hundred years; Oktoberfest in Munich did go ahead but it was massively scaled down.

September was a busy month for me as I embarked on my coaching course. I met a host of great people on the course who all wanted to become life coaches in their niche areas. However, my training came at a time that was strange and unknown. Gone were the days when you would experience training in a classroom environment; everything was now on Zoom and I spent a lot of time on my laptop, educating myself. It's crazy to think we built relationships and friendships through a screen, in some cases with people who were in different countries and different time zones.

Technology played a huge part in our interaction with others, particularly those who lived on their own. We relied on good internet connections to stream information, make video calls and play games, amongst other things. Our interactions were not the same as face-to-face communication and at times we would wonder what the person on the other end of the screen was really like. I remember the moment when I met someone in person for the first time after talking to them on Zoom – they were a lot shorter than I imagined! It was moments like that when you realise you only get to see a small portion of someone on a video call.

I saw some funny photos and read stories of people who were on work calls looking very presentable from the waist up but had their PJs, slippers and fluffy socks on. Because no one could see us below the waist, it made for some interesting 'business' attire. And what about those who were on the dating scene, using Zoom for speed dating? You'd be put in a Zoom room with someone for a few minutes to get to know them, then quickly moved into another room.

It was interesting to see the statistics on internet dating during the pandemic. An online article by Mary Ann Libert looked into how COVID had changed human relationships and social landscapes. A year-end report from Tinder found that from March 2020, the dating app broke its record for the most activity in a single day with more than 3 million swipes. Between March and May 2020, OKCupid saw a 700% increase in dates; on Bumble, video calls increased by 70%. It was evident that those on the lookout for love were taking the time to explore online avenues and utilising different platforms to meet people. However, the dating apps had to move quickly to incorporate functions that allowed for video calls and to create online dating events that opened up the pool of people looking for a suitable companion.

More and more deaths were being recorded across the world, mostly from COVID-19, but there were concerns around the validity of this data. People were still dying of other illnesses, such as cancer, but we didn't hear anything about the number of people dying of other causes as the news was heavily fixated on COVID-19. A report from the Office for National Statistics indicated that the leading cause of death in September 2020 in the UK was dementia and Alzheimer's disease; weirdly, coronavirus did not feature in the top 20 leading causes of death, either in England or Wales.

This was alarming to read, as the news stations were feeding us the news that COVID was a major cause of death. In September 2020, it was recorded that the global death toll surpassed one million. That is a huge number, but many of us didn't stop to think about people dying for other reasons. We hadn't ever had to be concerned with this previously – did we even know what those numbers were?

There were stories of individuals who lost loved ones during this time who commented on the fact that the pandemic took centre stage so those in hospital with other illnesses didn't get the same priority treatment. We were still in the thick of it, with so much more to come. We were living every day as it came, trying to embrace positivity and a vision of life getting back to normal as soon as possible. For some, this was not possible, and there was an increase in mental health problems and factors related to this, with many not having coping mechanisms in place.

We were yet to reach Christmas, a time of joy, a time with loved ones and a well-deserved break for many. What could this Christmas possibly bring us?

Chapter 13
Is This Over Yet?

October 2020, and we were slowly approaching Christmas. We'd had the most incredible summer, weather wise, and we were now going into the unknown of what we could and couldn't do as we approached the festive season.

COVID-19 cases continued to double in certain areas. The UK reported 22,961 cases in 24 hours but blamed this on a backlog of case reporting. We also heard that Donald Trump and the First Lady had tested positive for COVID-19, and the president was in hospital for a short period of time, leaving briefly for a drive-by appearance to wave at American citizens and show them he was doing okay. His comments shortly after being released from hospital sparked controversy as he compared COVID-19 to the flu, and Facebook and Twitter had to take action on posts by Trump in relation to this. YouTube also announced that it would remove anti-coronavirus vaccine content from its site, which resulted in a rise in other sites being used to spread anti-vaccine content.

President Trump was certainly making out that COVID-19 was less severe than we were being told. He also claimed the news of US cases rising was "fake conspiracy news" and that we shouldn't believe it. This put him firmly in the spotlight, and his social media accounts were monitored. However, it was clear that one of the most influential people in the world, the US president, was claiming the pandemic to be no more than normal flu. How this might be perceived by those in power was yet to be seen.

In Italy, face masks were made compulsory in outdoor spaces on 7th October. This ruling was seen to be really strict, particularly as many countries didn't impose outdoor restrictions, and it resulted in protests and looting, with the Italian police having to use teargas. For anyone who hasn't been to Italy, the streets are very enclosed in places and Italians love to sit outside and chat, so the risk of a virus spreading was possibly higher there. With my Italian background, it was sad to see how my family were living and the restrictions they had to abide by – but weren't we all?

On 12th October, the UK government announced a new three-tier system of restrictions in England, with many northern regions going into a higher tier. This made many of us feel even more isolated than others. It was crazy to think we could travel half an hour down the road and potentially be in another tier system with fewer restrictions. We were told that as the weather changed and it got colder, things could get a lot worse and cases may increase significantly.

France imposed a 9pm curfew on nine cities, including Paris, on 14th October. The thought that you couldn't go out after 9pm was absurd; people felt like they were being caged in their homes and there was no escape. In Ireland, tough restrictions were put in place to ban people from travelling more than 5km from their home, in another attempt to keep people indoors. Greece also followed with curfews in high-risk areas.

There was still no sign of a vaccine. Rumours suggested we wouldn't get one until Spring 2021. However, the UK ran the first coronavirus challenge trials, which infected young people with the virus to speed up the vaccine development. We are not sure how well this went, as there was little information on the outcome.

Towards the end of October, I was out with my family having a belated birthday meal for my mum when I had a really strong feeling that another lockdown was about to be imposed on us. I guess many thousands of people had the same thought as, on 24th October, tens of thousands of anti-lockdown protestors took to London to march against it. The media started to raise suspicions of another lockdown and this made us want to get to the shops and stock up again on all those essentials.

Towards the end of October, France and Germany imposed month-long lockdowns and Greece ordered regional lockdowns. We knew we could be next! Whilst having a lovely meal out on Hallowe'en, we heard that we were going into another lockdown on 5th November. The dreaded news was a big disappointment for the nation after having a small amount of freedom to do things, see family and engage with the outside world.

The four-week lockdown meant all non-essential retail outlets were closed along with pubs and restaurants, except for takeaways. Schools, universities and courts remained open. The reason for the lockdown was to prevent a "medical and moral disaster" for the NHS. It came after Europe passed 11 million COVID-19 cases, the UK passed 1 million confirmed cases, and the global death toll passed 1.2 million.

As we went into this second lockdown, I remember feeling a sense of despair. I was away from my family in Hertfordshire, I was on furlough from my job, and I was also trying to remain positive and upbeat as I embarked on more time by myself. Weirdly, I always had something in the diary, whether it be coaching related, listening to podcasts, watching webinars, or connecting with others. I took the time to really engage in self-learning and development and kept my fitness levels at a high standard by continuing my belly dance classes from home and doing HIIT workouts pretty much every day. I didn't want to pile on the pounds whilst at home, so I kept to a strict diet and didn't overindulge in alcohol or sweet treats. I was feeling at my best!

The furlough scheme was extended until the end of March, so I had some work to do in my HR role to support the team. It was a worrying time as people wondered whether their jobs would still be available and their employers would make it through, plus the added stress of trying to manage home schooling and looking after loved ones etc. It certainly tested our resilience; many were coping, but there were also many who were not.

A government study in November highlighted that depressive symptoms were at 12.5% pre-pandemic, rising to 22.6% in June and July 2020; in November and December, it rose again to 28.5%. It was evident that things were getting worse and levels of anxiety, depression and loneliness were rising month on month. With Christmas approaching, even more anxiety was afoot as we didn't quite know what we could do and who we could see; for those living on their own, it was a waiting game. A poll by the *Observer*/Opinium showed that UK citizens would prefer a Christmas lockdown over new January restrictions. This was certainly not my preferred option! Christmas is a special time of year for many families who want to get together; if anything, I would have expected it to be the opposite, with people preferring a January lockdown.

Later in November, a UK vaccine expert said it was expected that life should return to normal by Spring; Pfizer announced that its vaccine was 90% effective and Moderna said its vaccine was 94.5% effective. On 20th November, Matt Hancock, the UK Minister of Health, confirmed that the Pfizer vaccine would be rolled out from next month. Further data from Public Health England suggested that people with learning difficulties were six times more likely to die from coronavirus in England. This was a worrying fact to share with the public, inducing more anxiety and fear.

In the world of travel, Airport Councils Europe warned that 193 European airports could face insolvency within months if passenger traffic didn't get back to normal. Although some people did fly away on holiday whilst they could, many opted to stay at home because of the fear of contracting COVID-19. British Airways announced it was trialling a coronavirus testing system for passengers travelling to the UK from three American airports. This would give some reassurance to travellers who were frightened of the potential of being on a flight with someone with the virus. In contrast, on 12th November the first cruise ship to sail to the Caribbean since the pandemic began announced that it had five COVID-19 cases on board, with these individuals self-isolating in their cabins.

Towards the end of November, as we were slowly making our way through the four-week lockdown, the UK government provided details of the 'Covid Winter Plan'. It confirmed that there would be a three-tier system in England post-lockdown, and we waited for more information on this. On 24th November, Boris Johnson announced that families could bubble in three household groups from 23rd – 27th December. This brought much relief for those who were on their own and wanted to see their family at Christmas. I was one of those people and was thankful that I would be able to travel down to my mum and spend Christmas with her and my brother; I would certainly cherish these moments after nearly a year of being isolated from them.

I didn't know whether we would ever go back to 'normal' after living such an unreal life – one you only expect to see in the movies, one that has no resonance in this world. I could only remain optimistic and hopeful that life would be a new version of normal in the coming months.

Chapter 14
It's Christmas, and 2021 is Upon Us!

As we came out of the four-week lockdown we entered into a structured three-tier system, which gave us a little more freedom in the run-up to Christmas. There was lots going on at this time, from UK hospitals being told to prepare for a rollout of the COVID-19 vaccine in 10 days, to the UK securing 2 million doses of the Moderna vaccine. On 2nd December, the European Medicines Agency criticized the UK's decision to approve the Pfizer vaccine, arguing that the UK had prioritised speed over public health. This news came as many anti-vaxxers were vocal about how quickly a vaccine had been developed; they were saying it surely couldn't be safe – or that this was premeditated, and vaccines were already in development. This caused much speculation; however, thousands of people were keen to have their vaccine and would feel safer knowing they'd had it.

At this time, Facebook and Twitter announced they would remove false claims about the COVID-19 vaccine from their sites. The World Health Organization warned against complacency generated by the introduction of successful vaccines; it also warned the public that spending time with loved ones at Christmas was "not worth putting them or yourself at risk" and "Christmas celebrations could turn to sadness if people fail to be vigilant over the Christmas period" – which was not welcome news after the second lockdown in the UK.

We heard more about how other countries would roll out their vaccination programme; Canada had also approved the Pfizer vaccine and would begin on 14th December, while Germany would roll theirs out on 27th December. Whilst the UK had come out of lockdown, other countries had different ideas: Italy announced a national lockdown between 24-27th December, Austria followed, and Northern Ireland announced a six-week lockdown from Boxing Day.

On 19th December, the total number of COVID-19 cases globally passed 75 million and a new strain was found in the UK, which was thought to be 70% more transmissible. This, of course, caused more fear and worry. The relaxation period in the UK over Christmas was cut to just Christmas Day, and Scotland later announced that there would be a travel ban.

December was a month of change. The vaccines were being rolled out, and rules and restrictions were mixed depending on where you lived. However, fear was still prevalent as family members embarked on spending time together at Christmas. Those who were looking to travel abroad were informed by certain airlines that passengers were required to show a negative COVID-19 test before being allowed to travel, which brought its own worries.

By 21st December, the number of people who had received their first dose of the vaccine in the UK reached 500,000, which was astonishing considering it had only been rolled out at the start of the month. Later in December, the AstraZeneca vaccine was approved in the UK, with further doses being administered. At the same time, studies suggested there could be more COVID-19 deaths in the UK in the next six months than the whole of 2020 unless restrictions were increased.

The US went to great lengths to show US President-Elect

Joe Biden receiving his Pfizer vaccine live on television. He had very much been against Donald Trump's approach to the vaccines and COVID-19.

As Christmas approached, it felt like we all just wanted some cherished family time after the year we'd had. We were still living in the unknown and although restrictions were in place, we just wanted the freedom to enjoy whatever access we had to our loved ones. We were constantly being reminded that cases would increase if we were not careful, there would be more deaths if restrictions did not increase, and this did put a damper on things, particularly for those who were glued to the news and worried about what the media was feeding us.

Christmas 2020 was a quiet one for me and my family. We enjoyed a Zoom Christmas Eve party, dancing around the living room with other people dancing in their houses; it was the most excitement we'd had with other people in a long time. The season of goodwill felt strangely quiet and empty; however, I was so grateful for the time we spent together.

2021 was fast approaching and we were still in the dark about the future. What more would come of the vaccines? What further restrictions may we have? When would I get back to work? When would normal life resume? Would this ever end?

It was safe to say that the plot continued, with the UK government sharing great examples of following their own rules, further lockdowns, and more changes to our lives. Are you ready to embark on 2021: The Plot Thickens...?

Acknowledgements

Where do I start? I have a wealth of people to thank for supporting me in taking my idea for a book to it becoming reality. The idea of writing a book about COVID-19 came in 2020 when we were in the midst of a pandemic. It was steered by the very nature of our lives at that time. I thought it would be interesting to look back one day and remember the way life was in 2020, but I also wanted my book to be useful for the children of today and those of the future. My bigger vision is to share my book with schools to form part of history in years to come.

My first big thank you goes to my mum Angie and my brother Gero, who support me through everything I embark on. I have always come up with wacky ideas and my mum always laughs and comments on my craziness but also loves me for my drive and determination to achieve all I can in life. I couldn't do it without them.

I would also like to thank my partner Phil, who has been amazing. He always provided a listening ear when I needed to share my thoughts and ideas and, at times, those little moans when I hadn't quite figured things out.

I want to thank Fiona Lowe, a dear friend I used to work with. I embarked on her virtual DreamBuilder programme with two other friends, Surekha and Sanjeev. Together, we started to envision what we wanted in life – and this sparked the idea of my book. I want to thank them for supporting my vision and for all the little check-ins we had to start building the life we always wanted.

ACKNOWLEDGEMENTS

I also want to thank my co-workers, particularly Katherine, Paige and Janice, who I have worked with for six years. They have been supportive of everything I have been through and achieved throughout my career, and I am always able to share ideas and seek guidance when needed.

A big thank you goes to all my other friends and family: Victoria, Ian, Sheri, to name a few. There are too many names to mention; however, they have all played a part in giving me the confidence to write and making me accountable, and they have also provided me with ideas and encouragement.

Another thank you goes out to Kelly Swingler for her recommendation of a proofreader after having published her own book. She recommended Alison Thompson, The Proof Fairy, who proofread and edited my book and got it all set up and ready to be sold on Amazon. I couldn't have done the final piece without you: thank you.

I would also love to say a massive thank you to every one of you for buying and reading my book. Your support is greatly appreciated as you have allowed me to share my story and bring it to life. I hope this book brings you insight and allows you to reflect on your own life during the pandemic. What happened for you? What did you learn? What did you appreciate more at that time? What did you do differently after the pandemic?

I hope you will share this story with future generations, bringing them insight into a time that once was for millions of us across the world.

About the Author

Sophia Montagna was born in North London, England where she was brought up by her mother and grandparents. Although she was born in the UK, Sophia's parents are from Sicily so she started to learn Italian from a young age and continues to love speaking the language when she can.

As a child, Sophia owned a children's typewriter and briefcase, as she enjoyed writing. She loved reading books and pretending to teach her imaginary friends, and she envisioned being a speaker or trainer of some sort when she grew up.

Sophia certainly followed through on her vision as she embarked on a career in Human Resources, where she now has over 10 years' experience. Sophia thrives on supporting others to reach their potential within their careers as well as in their lives. She has been a public speaker at events as well as on panels, is a trainer/coach and continues to enjoy learning and developing, particularly within the areas of psychology and wellbeing. She is a Mental Health First Aider, a Chief Happiness Officer, a life coach and NLP practitioner.

Alongside her passion for helping others, Sophia loves to be creative and enjoys making her own greetings cards. She is active in her spare time and enjoys belly dancing, cycling and swimming.

References

World Economic Forum (2020). *Key milestones in the spread of Coronavirus pandemic*. Accessed 24 April 2020 through https://www.weforum.org/agenda/2020/04/coronavirus-spread-covid19-pandemic-timeline-milestones/

Business Insider (2020). *Both the new coronavirus and SARS outbreaks likely started in Chinese 'wet markets'. Historic photos show what the markets looked like.* Accessed 24 April 2020 through https://www.businessinsider.com/wuhan-coronavirus-chinese-wet-market-photos-2020-1

World Health Organisation (2020). *SARS (Severe Acute Respiratory Syndrome)*. Accessed 26 April 2020 through https://www.emro.who.int/health-topics/severe-acute-respiratory-syndrome/

Devex (2020). *COVID-19 – A timeline of the coronavirus outbreak*. Accessed 24 April 2020 through https://www.devex.com/news/covid-19-a-timeline-of-the-coronavirus-outbreak-104923/amp

BBC News (2020). *Two new cases confirmed in UK*. Accessed 26 April 2020 through https://www.bbc.co.uk/news/uk-51656609.amp

Science Mag (2020). *Coronavirus infections keep mounting after cruise ship fiasco in Japan*. Accessed 26 April 2020 through https://www.science.org/content/article/coronavirus-infections-keep-mounting-after-cruise-ship-fiasco-japan

BBC News (2020). *How NHS Nightingale was built in just 9 days*. Accessed 29 April 2020 through https://www.bbc.co.uk/news/health-52125059.amp

The Guardian (2020). *He's just a wonderful man – How Captain Tom became a superstar fundraiser*. Accessed 2 May 2020 through https://amp.theguardian.com/world/2020/may/01/hes-just-a-wonderful-man-how-captain-tom-became-a-superstar-fundraiser

BBC News (2020). *Coronavirus – Eight things that have kept us going in lockdown*. Accessed 2 May 2020 through https://www.bbc.co.uk/news/uk-52578358.amp

BBC News (2020). *Lockdown and weight gain – should you worry?* Accessed 4 May 2020 through https://www.bbc.co.uk/news/uk-52578358.amp

The Guardian (2020). *Half of British adults felt anxious about COVID-19 lockdown*. Accessed 4 May 2020 through https://amp.theguardian.com/society/2020/may/04/half-of-british-adults-felt-anxious-about-covid-19-lockdown

BBC News (2020). *How lockdown is being lifted across Europe*. Accessed 8 May 2020 through https://www.bbc.co.uk/news/explainers-52575313.amp

Hewitts (2020). *Covid-19: Lockdown leads to increase in divorce enquiries*. Accessed 8 May 2020 through https://www.stewartslaw.com/news/why-have-divorce-rates-increased-during-the-covid-19-pandemic/

The Guardian (2020). *Clean air in Europe during lockdown leads to 11,000 fewer deaths.* Accessed 12 May 2020 through https://amp.theguardian.com/environment/2020/apr/30/clean-air-in-europe-during-lockdown-leads-to-11000-fewer-deaths

The Guardian (2020). *Rishi Sunak confirms furlough scheme to be gradually withdrawn.* Accessed 12 May 2020 through https://amp.theguardian.com/politics/2020/may/29/rishi-sunak-confirms-coronavirus-furlough-scheme-to-be-gradually-withdrawn

BBC News (2020). *Coronavirus: UK interest rates cut to lowest ever.* Accessed 16 May 2020 through https://www.bbc.co.uk/news/business-51962982.amp

BBC News (2020). *Coronavirus: Domestic violence 'increases' globally during lockdown.* Accessed 20 June 2020 through https://www.bbc.co.uk/news/uk-55073229.amp

Sky News (2020). *Coronavirus crisis delivers 'biggest' income shock since the mid 1970s.* Accessed 17 August 2020 through https://news.sky.com/story/coronavirus-crisis-delivers-biggest-income-shock-since-the-mid-1970s-12032630

The Guardian (2020). *UK Coronavirus job losses: the latest data on redundancies and furloughs.* Access 17 August 2020 through https://www.theguardian.com/world/2020/jul/31/uk-coronavirus-job-losses-the-latest-data-on-redundancies-and-furloughs

REFERENCES

Euro News (2020). *Coronavirus job cuts: Which companies in Europe are slashing their workforces because of COVID-19*. Accessed 17 August 2020 through https://www.euronews.com/business/2020/07/24/coronavirus-job-cuts-which-companies-in-europe-are-slashing-their-workforces-because-of-co

Sky News (2020). *Coronavirus: Working from home costs add up as more spent on tea and biscuits*. Accessed 17 August 2020 through https://news.sky.com/story/coronavirus-working-from-home-costs-add-up-as-more-spent-on-tea-and-biscuits-12033104

The Guardian (2020). *Protestors march for fair pay for nurses and other NHS staff*. Accessed 10th April 2023 through http://amp.theguardian.com/society/2020/aug/08/hundreds-march-fair-pay-nhs-nurses-coronavirus

British Foreign Policy Group (2021). *COVID-19 Timeline*. Accessed 10 April 2023 through http://bfpg.couk/2020/04/covid-19-timeline/

Scientific American (2024). *Nine COVID-19 Myths That Just Won't Go Away*. Accessed 28 January 2024 through https://www.scientificamerican.com/article/nine-covid-19-myths-that-just-wont-go-away/

BBC News (2024). *The Chinese doctor who tried to warn others about coronavirus*. Accessed 28 January 2024 through https://www.bbc.com/news/world-asia-china-51364382.amp

Mary Ann Libert (2024). *How COVID Has Changed Online Dating – And What Lies Ahead.* Accessed 28 January 2024 through https://liebertpub.com/doi/10.1089/cyber.2021.29219.editorial

Printed in Great Britain
by Amazon